Notes on

ted Poems

.H. Auden

cational London and Sydney

First published 1978 by Pan Books Ltd
Cavaye Place, London SW10 9PG
1 2 3 4 5 6 7 8 9
© Graham Handley 1978
ISBN 0 330 50120 8
Filmset in Great Britain by
Northumberland Press Ltd, Gateshead, Tyne and Wear
Printed and bound by
Richard Clay (The Chaucer Press) Ltd, Bungay Suffolk

Contents

These notes are based on the Faber paperback
edition of *Selected Poems* by W. H. Auden, but
references are made to each individual poem,
so the Notes may be used with any edition of
the poems

To the student

W. H. Auden's works reflect a wide learning and contain a range of reference from the esoteric to the private joke. He was a genuine and lovable eccentric, in his later years pottering about in slippers and dressing-gown, enjoying his wine and crosswords, always paying meticulous attention to time. He was both serious and irreverent, and to appreciate his poems we have to respond to his mood, his concerns, and often the tantalizing acrostics of his language. No critical commentary on Auden's works can provide all the answers – only an invitation to participate in the enjoyment of intellectual exercise afforded by a poet of sensitivity and compassion. Auden responded to the geological pulse-beat of his early years, to the political hammer-blows of the nineteen-thirties and the spiritual concerns of his time.

A complete glossary on Auden would run to the length of a Shakespeare Concordance; what is more important, it would destroy the name and nature of his poetry. His work should be read, as all poetry should be read, for the experience, the theme, the technique, the associations set up, all the contributory facets which make a poem a unique work of art.

The poet and his work

Wystan Hugh Auden was born in 1907, the son of a York doctor. The following year the family moved to Birmingham. After leaving preparatory school (where he first met Christopher Isherwood) Auden went on to Gresham's School in Norfolk. It was there, at the age of fifteen, that he first realized that he would be a poet. This early sense of vocation led to his first venture into print in 'Public School Verse' some two years later. In 1925 he went to Christ Church College, Oxford, acquiring there the appreciation of Old and Middle English which is so evident in the rhythms and constructions of much of his own verse. There too he was subjected to the wave of reaction which followed the publication of T. S. Eliot's *The Waste Land* (1922). Auden edited *Oxford Poetry* and then had his first poems printed privately by Stephen Spender in 1928. The following year was spent in Germany, where he came under the rather different influences of Brecht, Freud and the German theatre and songs. All these contributed to the sharpening of his sense of dramatic and poetic possibilities, both of which were to be explored in the ensuing years. In Berlin he renewed his close friendship with Christopher Isherwood, who was also to turn his experiences to good literary account.

Initially some of Auden's poems were rejected by T. S. Eliot, but he published *Paid on Both Sides: the charade* in 1930, and later in the same year Faber and Faber issued his *Poems, 1930*. For the next four years Auden was teaching at an Academy in Scotland, but he produced *The Orators* in 1932 and began to write reviews on a variety of subjects. In these comparatively early years his questing nature was revealed in his dramatic association with the Group Theatre (witness *The Dance of Death* in 1933) and his writing for *Scrutiny*, which was then regarded as a magazine producing radical literary criticism. In retrospect, this energy seems remarkable; in 1935, in collaboration with Isherwood, he wrote *The Dog Beneath the Skin*, contributed his own commentary to an excellent documentary film, *Night Mail*, and, with John Garrett, edited *The Poet's Tongue*, an anthology which has become a classic deserving, in the eyes of some, to rank with Palgrave's *Golden Treasury*.

The year 1935 brought multiple activities in life and literature – for example, marriage to Erika Mann, daughter of the great German writer Thomas Mann. Auden, branded a left-wing intellectual by so many of his contemporaries, here displayed a paradoxical sense of chivalry, for he did not know the lady, and married her in order to provide her with a passport so that she could escape from Nazi Germany. He wrote *The Ascent of F.6*, a play, with Isherwood, and went to Iceland with a fellow-poet, Louis MacNeice. Faber and Faber published their *Letters from Iceland* in the following year. The volume, issued to Auden's disgust under the title of *Look, Stranger*, was followed in 1937 by *Spain*, while in 1938 he and Isherwood went to China to report on the war with Japan; this record was published as *Journey to a War* in 1939. Together they also wrote *On the Frontier*, while Auden's publishers issued his *Selected Poems*. Early in 1939 Auden and Isherwood left England and subsequently settled in the United States. *Another Time* came out in 1940, dedicated to Chester Kallman, with whom Auden was to spend the rest of his life. Articles and reviews continued to absorb much of his time but during the next two years he found time to teach at the University of Michigan. Throughout the rest of his life he was engaged in casual but concentrated teaching elsewhere in America.

For the Time Being was published in America in 1944 and in England the following year; it contained 'The Sea and the Mirror', prominently featured in this selection, while his

Collected Poetry (published in America) appeared in 1945. In the following year he became an American citizen. In 1947 he published *The Age of Anxiety*, which was dedicated to John Betjeman. He was awarded a Pulitzer Prize in 1948. 1950 saw the *Collected Shorter Poems* and *The Enchafed Flood*, 1951 *Nones* and, with Chester Kallman, the libretto for Stravinsky's *The Rake's Progress*, which was performed in Venice. Throughout this period the articles and reviews from his pen flowed on, and in addition he held several American college and university appointments. In 1954 he was elected to the American Academy of Arts and Letters. *The Shield of Achilles* was published in 1955, and from 1956 until 1961 Auden was Professor of Poetry at Oxford. He continued to be a prolific reviewer and in 1958 the Penguin selection of his poems was issued. *Homage to Clio* was published in 1960, he was made an honorary fellow of Christ Church, Oxford, while that most individual book of essays, *The Dyer's Hand*, came out in England in 1963. In 1965 another volume of poems, *About the House*, containing 'Thanksgiving for a Habitat', was published.

The last phase of Auden's life showed an even greater increase in output, and the collected *Academic Graffiti* were written between 1952 and 1970. *City Without Walls* appeared in 1967, *Epistle to a Godson* in 1969, and *Thank You, Fog*, the posthumous volume, in 1974, the year after the poet's death.

This chronological introduction has been written in some detail because Auden is a major poet and because the reader of this Study Aid may not be confining himself to the Selected Poems. A general appraisal of Auden's verse and his achievements may help to serve as a prelude to a more detailed consideration of his writings. When the history of English poetry in the twentieth century comes to be written, Auden's name will figure prominently and with distinction for the sheer virtuosity of his talent and the breadth of his learning. He was a poet who grew with his time, reflected it and yet transcended it, always open to the challenge of fresh intellectual experience. Friend and collaborator of Isherwood, left-wing associate of Day Lewis and Spender, appreciator of Louis MacNeice, paradoxically conservative enough to praise Betjeman, Auden's mind is perhaps the most dazzling of them all.

The early Auden was an intellectually angry young man, aware of the menaces of his time but rational and scientific in his interests as well as literary. The abiding influence of his doctor father is apparent in his early work, and linked with this is his absorption of basic psychology, the theories of which were to inform his verse. Monroe Spears notes Auden's interest in fantasy, particularly the fantasies of Norse legends and literature which had attracted him in youth. But between 1922 and 1928, when his first poems appeared, Auden read widely in English poetry, and this volume of reading gave him a facility, derivative and in part imitative, which he was to employ to good effect throughout his life. His geological interests are often evident, but there is an allusiveness and obscurity about some of his early writing which makes him 'difficult' for the student. Auden has a fine sense of the *sound* of his own verse, from the sonorous quality of 'The Wanderer' to the softness of 'Lullaby' ('Lay your sleeping head, my love').

In *Letters from Iceland* the verse to Lord Byron takes the reader on a literary and very funny romp through the author's own personal reactions to events of the past and the present, an audacious and individual performance evocative of the nineteen-thirties and Auden himself. These early poems have a satirical flavour, with slanted irony at the nature of the bourgeois society and its attitudes and part of Auden's method is that of deliberate ambiguity. This area of double interpretation, of a poet existing on more than one level, is testimony both to his intellect and to his astute organization of word resonance and association. In his early work too he establishes his own variants of the sonnet, some English in form, others derived from the influence and practice of the German poet Rainer Maria Rilke. *Selected Poems* contains the fifth ode of *The Orators*, with its old soldier's tone and advice masking the important issues of conformity and conflict, and the epilogue also appears.

In the 1930s Auden's impact on his contemporaries was great; by early 1933 Hitler had seized power in Germany and Auden, like Isherwood, had witnessed what might be called the prelude to prolonged persecution: victimization, terror, racism, the calculated deployment of dictatorship. But unlike so many of his contemporaries Auden did not become a Communist or seek to use political ends, though his powerful poem *Spain 1937* certainly has political overtones. The plays, however, are concerned with their time. Auden was one of the founder members of the Group Theatre, and *The Dance of Death* (1933) involved the audience in a way which would be thoroughly approved today. *The Dog Beneath the Skin* is full of life, farce and a shrewd look at the establishment and, more particularly, at Fascism. *The Ascent of F.6* was produced in 1936 and has a strong psychological emphasis; one of the songs, 'The Witnesses', appears in *Collected Poems*.

Auden used song – popular and blues, for example – throughout his writing career and the nineteen-thirties saw his peak achievements in terms of adaptation and parody. He became so adept at transforming his material that he was able to use it again in a different context without loss of force. The ironic conception inherent in most of the songs is markedly present in 'Autumn Song' (*Selected Poems*), where the attack is once more on the middle classes, the 'Christopher Robin' type song being inverted to show the child growing up into a carefully constructed, well-ordered world. Auden was at that time becoming more interested in religion, and by 1940 there is evidence of his virtual acceptance of Christianity. In following this pattern of development Auden was tracing a movement common to many: that from early radicalism in morality, politics or religion to conservatism in later maturity. This is mentioned in passing, since *Selected Poems* by-passes *For the Time Being* and continues with *The Sea and the Mirror*. Here the subtitle (A Commentary on Shakespeare's *The Tempest*) is important, and the forms in which the various characters speak are a further indication of Auden's versatility. The play is over, and each character, pre-existing in his closed world of performance, is supposedly stepping into the real world of life. Thus the sequence deals with art and life, just as *The Tempest* does.

A number of poems from *The Shield of Achilles* occur in the Faber selection and the poem from which this sequence takes its title is a work of splendid irony. It is examined in some detail in the summaries and textual notes, for what was represented in Homer's *Iliad* is transformed by Auden into a representation of modern life, a nightmare indictment of man's inhumanity to man. Other poems in this group follow suit, 'Fleet Visit' being a particularly good example, with the American sailors carrying nothing of the heroic stature of their Homeric counterparts. The *Horae Canonicae* are religious in basis, varied in execution, while *Nones* focuses upon the Crucifixion. The last selection here is taken from *About the House*, being based on Auden's own home in Austria, with one poem given to each of the rooms; perhaps the most significant is the elegiac treatment of his friend Louis MacNeice, who died in 1963.

Auden is neither follower nor leader but a chooser, and the choice of poems in this selection follows the circle of his major concerns and interests over the course of his writing career. Auden is unquestionably one of the greatest poets of our time; his work will survive critical changes of heart and at the same time will continue to represent a major achievement over some forty-five years of a century undistinguished in major poets.

Further reading

The Poetry of W. H. Auden: the disenchanted island Monroe K. Spears (Oxford University Press)
A Reader's Guide to W. H. Auden John Fuller (Thames and Hudson)
Journey to a War W. H. Auden and Christopher Isherwood (Faber)

Summaries of poems and textual notes

All references in the summaries and notes which follow below are taken from the *Selected Poems* by W. H. Auden, a Faber paperback first published in 1968. The edition used for this commentary was published in 1976.

The secret agent

Written in January 1928. It is in the form of an unrhymed sonnet, clearly divided into the two quatrains which form the octave, with the complete break into the sestet. The tone is conversational, the interpretation revealing an additional as well as a superficial meaning which, as will be seen, is typical of Auden. Auden's Old English affiliations (here he is fresh from reading English at Oxford) are more fully exemplified in *The Wanderer*. Here the spy is betrayed and his foraging work ignored, while in the sestet there is the strong suggestion that human contact ('The street music') is essential for those who have been deprived, forcefully or voluntarily, of it. The sexual interpretation would obviously see the octave as phallic and the sestet as a comment on loneliness.

Control of the passes Strategy.
bogus guide False information.
wires Telegrammed information.
street music i.e. it represents contact with humanity.
Reproached the night Cursed his loneliness.
Parting easily i.e. from his dream of love.

The Watershed

Written in August 1927, this poem has a significant title since the definition of it is 'a line of separation between waters flowing to different rivers' or, figuratively, a turning point. The writer contemplates the derelict mines, ponders on their past workings, touches on a story (two miners), considers his own position of non-communication with the area (he is the 'stranger') and is aware of nature (the hare in the final lines scenting danger). Thus the past and the present are linked in this conversational poem, the blank verse lines conveying the desolation of the scene and the memories which it gives rise to, but the poet, the contemplator, can have no part of this, for by position and inheritance he is different. The hare, too, is separated, but the word with which the poem ends – 'danger' – is a key one, for it refers to the danger in which the miners worked, the dangers lurking in nature and, perhaps, the danger inherent in man's dissociation from man.

washing-floors Where the ore is washed.

Snatches Pieces, sections, probably broken.

comatose In a state of prolonged unconsciousness.

workings Mining excavations.

some acts are chosen Remembered, selected by the mind.

the fells Stretches of high moorland.

in wooden shape Note the ironic associations with the coffin.

went to ground Here the associations are with animals – miners burrow as animals do.

They wake no sleeper Because no one is employed there any more.

unbaffled The implication is that nature continues, resumes its cycle although man may change.

Ears noise The hare in fear.

O where are you going

This was published as the Epilogue to *The Orators* (1932), 'a surrealist anatomy of a country in crisis' according to Fuller, who later observes that its comparison in terms of significance to *The Waste Land* is justified. Here the quatrains with heavy alliteration and onomatopoeic effects, the use of the ballad form, the consonance and assonance, all justify Monroe Spears' assertion that it is 'a little parable in the form of a riddle', while its derivation from the folk-song 'The Cutty Wren' has also been noted. The invocatory 'O' is a favourite device of Auden's, as is the use of real or simulated dialogue in a complex technical exercise which is redolent of fear, the build-up of menace. The atmosphere is that of the nightmare, dangers, horrors, fears, the supernatural, omens – all appear in a poem which has a medieval quality. Despite all the warnings and fears of the first speaker (reader-fearer-horror) the second speaker (rider-farer-hearer) decides to accept the challenge.

midden Dunghill or refuse heap.
the tall return The spirits of the dead.
lacking What you fail to notice.
bird ... twisted Note the nightmare effect – birds are frequently signs of ill-omen.
the figure ... The spot on your skin The subconscious fears which we have.
As he left them there As he acts, as distinct from those left behind, who don't act. The technique throughout this poem may be compared with 'O What is That Sound' on p.17.

The wanderer

This was published in 1932, and harks back to the Old English poem of the same name, though the first line comes from the Middle English *Sawles Warde*, while the 'doom' referred to is to be equated with the judgement of God. The theme — that of exile and loneliness — is compellingly explored in blank verse lines of varying length which again have the rhythmic lilt and form of the Anglo-Saxon about them. It is a moving poem, full of fine images, both visual and human. The geography of the poem — the nature of the landscape, the isolation, the correspondence of mood to this — is admirable. The heavy rhythms are themselves evocative of fate, though the final verse strikes a note of optimism in the possible return of the wanderer, though the air of menace is still prevalent.

sea-dingle A deep dell.

day-wishing flowers Fine unobtrusive personification in this double-barrelled coinage — the flowers 'wish' to appear.

place-keepers A coinage for 'those who remain'.

chat A bird — note the comparison between man and nature in loneliness.

stone-haunting Another fine coinage, linked here with 'unquiet' to convey isolation and fear.

making another love The implication is that it is not the 'natural' love of man and wife — it may refer to war or money for example.

tiger's leap Note the use of the unfamiliar in this context to indicate the sudden ambush and physical violence.

ruin ... stain Auden's use of the half-rhyme, and a favourite image too.

returning ... approaching ... leaning Note that the effect of the -ing words is to convey 'continuing', and that the whole verse carries an allegorical meaning — the wanderer is representative of all men, or of mankind.

Ode

Written in 1932, another part of *The Orators*, justly celebrated and included in the *Selected Poetry* of 1958. It was later headed 'Which Side am I supposed to be on?' and is written in sixteen regular six-lined stanzas, two shorter lines in every verse, for the most part without rhyme. The central theme is war, the first verse focusing on its aspects of ambush, for example, the second on the past, the third almost a parody of a film sequence with the 'agent' collapsing. The conversational tone is very marked at this stage. The next two verses deal with readiness in the sense of the recruit and the old soldier, but the enemy is not defined, 'the aggressor/No one you know'. The next verses deal with the development of the militaristic tradition – boyish games, Daddy away fighting, prayers, blessing by the Bishop, parades, the whole paraphernalia of family and community preparation. The enemy is both within (because of this preparation) and without, and Auden passes on to an account of the Seven Deadly Sins, all couched in military terminology which is itself a condemnation of a way of life. But the final two verses bring all the preparations to actuality, that is to the fact of war itself as distinct from the preparations, the parodies, the boyish games.

in the working of copper Mining, making things from copper – coins for example.

The maned lion common A reference to the past, to the early times when man had to protect himself against this 'enemy'.

The pillar dug ... The sack of a city Archeological excavations which enable man to trace events of the distant past.

They got me Cliché phrase of the American gangster film. It is part of Auden's enigmatic style to juxtapose past and present throughout this, and other, poems.

Our hope Ironic. The young men are the hope of the future, but the two words recall the hymn traditionally associated with peace after war – 'O God our help in Ages past/Our hope ...'.

already a tiger Note the echo of the 'maned lion' in this boyish game.

To stand with the wine-dark conquerors Again the language of the past to underline the continuity of military preparation – 'wine-dark' is a favourite epithet of Homer, author of *The Iliad* and *The Odyssey*.

While in a great rift This whole verse deals with those who have been defeated.

There's Wrath The first of the deadly sins personified, all of which are defined in military terms, thus equating sin and war.

to lying/As husband true Another clipped turn of phrase which appears to mean that husbands lie to deceive their jealous (envious) wives. But very often meaning in Auden cannot be pinned down; it is the cumulative effect of his statements which is important and which establishes the poetic effect of the poem.

Acedia Sloth.

There are faces there The implication is of the enemy within, of spying and betrayal, common in the Germany of the nineteen-thirties where children were encouraged to betray their parents.

squat Pictish tower Built by the ancient people in North Britain.

Death to the squealer Again the use of nineteen-thirties American slang. A squealer is one who betrays a fellow criminal to the police.

Inverted commas i.e. sarcastically.

culverts Channels, here probably for electric cables.

the bunting signals Flags sending coded messages.

Legend

This is the chorus from *The Dog Beneath the Skin* where Alan Norman finds himself the man appointed to go in search of the missing Sir Francis Crewe. It is therefore a 'quest' poem, a lyrical mode of expression. The invocation is that he may be accompanied in his search by 'Love', which will protect him and see him through all difficulties until he comes near the end, when 'Love' must be sacrificed, so that reality – freed from enchantment – will prevail, and he will find what he searched for. The lyrical mood is sustained throughout and the whole has the tone and treatment of a fairy tale, the enchantment ultimately giving way to reality, the discovery of 'the dog beneath the skin'.

Corrosive seas i.e. because they can destroy him.
The common phrase i.e. the words which will see him through.
But disenchanted i.e. he has won through to reality.

O what is that sound

Assigned by Mendelson to 1932, this is in ballad-form with the dialogue built into each verse; an air of timeless menace is created; although the poem could be assigned to historical time, the tone is modern and conversational, with a swinging pendulum of question and answer, though it is not quite clear who is the traitor and who the betrayed. Repetition, the variation of the feminine (two-syllable) rhymes and, above all perhaps, the oblique comment on the menace, fear and violence of Auden's own times, make this a fine piece of atmospheric writing. The ballads of old celebrated the traditions and legends of the time and of time past, but here there is a frightening realism (see the final verse) which gives the whole poem an ironic quality. There is a terrifying implication of determined rape and pillage, a mirror held up to the dictatorships of Hitler and Mussolini, the rule by coercion, persecution and fear.

drumming, drumming Note that the repetition is insistent, unflagging, as inevitable as the coming of the soldiers.
dear Ironic, in view of the betrayal.
manoeuvres In the thirties, the word was synonymous with threat, the coming attack on or coercion of a smaller nation.
kneeling To keep out of sight and to pray.
doctor's ... parson ... farmer Note that these references encompass the stable elements of the community – but all are under threat by the forces of dictatorship.
But I must be leaving A very effective use of the colloquial – again Auden is using the film cliché to show the cheapness of human conduct.
it's Notice the terrible *impersonality* this implies – man in the mass loses his humanity and kills or rapes as part of the machine process of dictatorship.

As I walked out one evening

First published in the *New Statesman* in 1938, a folksong ballad form is employed again; there are splendid contrasts of past and present, of plenty and of the changes wrought by time. The tone is as clipped and yet as wide-ranging and enigmatic as usual. The idea of past and present, or of seeing one thing in terms of another, is shown in the first verse, while the second speaks of a timeless love, emphasized to distortion in verse three, which has all the exaggeration of the popular song, which turns time and morality upside down. The pattern of terrestrial and cosmic change, which has a kind of reversed nursery rhyme tone to it, is continued in verses four and five. The first cynical note is struck in verse six, which stresses that time measures love as it measures all things, while verse seven, with its heavy, surrealistic personification, further underlines that love is a 'snatched' rather than a permanent thing. The next three verses focus on modern life – headaches, changes in nature, dances, worry – and the brimming river (life at the full) has become the dirty water of the basin, or sordid, habitual reality. The tenth verse opens with the widest natural imagery in contrast to the constricted nature of life – glaciers, desert, lane – but the nightmare reversal of the nursery rhyme continues, with all the simple morality of such tales and songs turned upside down. Doom, nightmare doom, is sounded in the next two verses, with the implication that life is twisted and tortured, and that love is lust rather than purity. The last verse returns to the river which, like life, flows on.

fields of harvest wheat Note the description of plenty, but carrying with it the suggestion of changes in time, for fields become streets.

brimming river … arch of the railway Auden is deliberately telescoping time, so that past and present are juxtaposed in his verse.

Till China and Africa meet Auden has ironically captured the distortion of the popular song and the nursery rhyme as well.

The seven stars ... geese Again the nursery rhyme tone.

The Flower of the Ages The ideal, what is perfect.

Time ... Nightmare ... Justice Note the personification, deliberately used to avoke the reality of experience, whether in the conscious or subconscious mind. The implication is that the truths of life will find you out.

the appalling snow The use of the word 'appalling' has been compared to the pun-like effect achieved by Blake through 'appalled', with its suggestion of what is terrifying and the 'pall' of death.

threaded dances ... brilliant bow Changes in time destroy the beauty or achievement of the moment.

glacier ... desert ... lane to the land of the dead All powerful suggestions to the subconscious of what 'you've missed' – exploration, travel etc. Perhaps, too, make believe, the world of the imagination.

Where the beggars raffle The reversal of all the nursery rhymes – Jack getting on with the Giant, purity becoming loose living, Jill ready for sexual adventure. The tone is mockingly ironical – the truths of childhood are not the truths of life.

Although you cannot bless The line reminds us of Coleridge's Ancient Mariner who, having killed the albatross, cannot bless either.

your crooked neighbour ... crooked heart Another nursery rhyme turned into an ironic comment on the limitations of human nature.

Song of the beggars

Published in May 1935, this is a poem in six verses, the first three rhyming loosely, the second three directly, each verse ending with a two-line refrain. It is an allegory on the truth of life – we can't have what we ask for, just as beggars can't be rich. As each verse deals with one facet of the beggars' wishes, so Auden is dealing with one aspect of life in terms of wish and fulfilment. Verse one has the theme of social position, society, status, but the ridiculous names (Lobcock, Asthma) indicate the ironic tone. In verse two the emphasis is on the sexual, Garbo being the cinematic equivalent of the historical and legendary Cleopatra; verse three switches to horses and gambling, the fourth to getting away from it all, the fifth is an attack on the capitalist way of life, the sixth an indictment of the complacency of religion, the fact that spirituality cures no physical evils.

Lobcock Bumpkin, clown, fool.
Garbo's Greta Garbo, Swedish film actress who went to Hollywood and is regarded as one of the great 'stars' of all time.
Cleopatra's The beautiful Egyptian who captivated, among others, Mark Antony. She lived from 69–30 BC.
a feather ocean A bed.
foresee their places The results of the races.
to be a deck i.e. a boat on which to sail away.
pokes from a flower Note the artistic, surrealistic effect of this.
to have no legs at all The implication is that being partly incapacitated is the same as being fully crippled.

Autumn song

Published in 1936, this poem has obvious echoes and affinities with Blake's *Songs of Innocence and Experience*. These are seen in the form and in the duality of emphasis. The tone is light, but the undercurrent is serious; the first verse, highly satirical in tone, marks the passage of time between birth and death, while the second ponders on pettiness, loneliness, frustration in life, and the third considers the standards and attitudes and their influence from the past on the present. The fourth verse is concerned with the worlds of spirits and spirituality, but the images are of trolls and the birds, like God, are silent. In the final verse the movement is towards what 'might have been', perhaps a definition of the lack of fulfilment in life or art.

Able ... Derelict Notice how Auden makes use of direct contrast to underline loneliness and frustration.

Alack An archaic word expressing regret or surprise, and thus appropriately used here to indicate the attitudes of the past.

Trolls Supernatural beings in Scandinavian mythology, frequently mischievous.

Owl and nightingale The predatory and the beautiful.

the Mountains of Instead Effectively heavy personification to underline the cynical observation.

Roman Wall blues

This appeared first as part of a radio script in 1937 on *Hadrian's Wall*. It is an evocation of place, loneliness, the slow passage of time, a comment on human nature and its change-lessness throughout history. The seven rhyming couplets are conversational and colloquial in tone, further evidence of Auden's ability to use a variety of forms. The focus is on the lot of the soldier regardless of historical time.

Tungria In what is now Belgium.

Piso's a Christian, he worships a fish An oblique reference to Christ, one of whose titles gave their inititals to make the word ichthus, Greek for fish.

When I'm a veteran Perhaps the implication is that he won't be on active service as he is now.

Lullaby

A beautiful lyric, the high watermark of Auden's early achievement, first published in *New Writing* in 1937. It is written in the form of four ten-line verses, with rhymes and half-rhymes abounding and together forming the elements of its title. The first verse explores the night of happiness spent together, but built into the lyrical expression of this happiness is the recognition of the changes wrought by life, and of the transitory nature of experience. The second verse is itself transitional, for it moves from the contemplation of sensual love to the nature of spiritual love, a love which transcends the human and is concerned with the ecstasy of spiritual knowledge. Contrasts and parallels are used here to emphasize the analogous aspects of such a love. The third verse deals with the present – its completeness and beauty, the forces which seek to undermine it, the value the lovers should place upon it.

The theme of love runs through the final verse, with the recurrence to the sensual and the spiritual seen as coherent, related parts of essential life experience. The poem is rich in alliteration, assonance and consonance, all of which contribute to the lyrical quality. There is an underlying seriousness running through the whole length of the poem which makes it somewhat untypical of the lyrical form; but what it shares with many fine lyrics is the fact that it is general and particular, personal and universal in its application.

faithless arm Transferred epithet, quietly ironic, since the placing of the word here next to another which it does not qualify effectively underlines the unromantic nature of the poem.

fevers Perhaps of the mind as well as the body.

Mortal, guilty i.e. real, capable of error, but essentially human.

abstract insight ... carnal ecstasy Love of the spiritual, of God, is seen in terms equivalent to those used of physical love. Thus love, an integral theme in Auden's poetry, is here defined in terms of its dimensions.

On the stroke of midnight pass The use of time to indicate change – a new day will arrive – but adding too the associations of story and legend to reinforce the idea of inevitability, here an echo of *Cinderella*.

Eye and knocking heart may bless/Find our mortal world enough To be capable of experience, whether fearful or happy, indicates the capacity to love and be loved.

By the involuntary powers Whatever may happen to you that you yourself have not willed.

As he is

This consists of seven verses of eight lines each with alternate lines rhyming, some directly, some loosely. In the first verse man is seen in contradistinction to nature, for he is 'Loud in his hope and anger', while in verse two we see the development of his imperialistic role – either as soldier or missionary or photographer (or film-maker) spying out the secrets of lands and nature. A poignant note is sounded at the end of this verse, however, for we are told that he is 'Able at times to cry'. This gives place in verse three to the argument that men has been set against nature by tradition and its influences, the ties of family constraint.

Verse four elaborates upon this by showing how man is conditioned by the force of heredity, for although he grows to manhood he is unable to penetrate the 'tall imposing tower' of human nature, for it is 'locked' to him by virtue of his inherited incapacity. His time is divided between obsession on the one hand and loneliness on the other, and however elevated his vision he does not succeed in achieving it, though he has ideals which look beyond the 'beauties' about him. In the sixth verse the contrast in man's nature is represented as that between the tigress and the lamb, stressed in images drawn from heraldry.

The last verse shows man, because of his vulnerability, betrayed by transitory things, for example false ideals, but he must suffer defeats and grief before he finally defeats grief itself. The poem is therefore an allegory on the journey of man through life, with the idea that ultimately the forces within him must be reconciled.

noiseless hunger ... clandestine tide ... high fever Note this
   sequence of fine metaphors which convey life force in terms of
   appetite, movement and ecstasy.
the deliberate man An ironic appraisal of the fact that man has
   freedom of will.
and fairer That are naturally beautiful.

a living gun Economical way of defining man's capacity to destroy.

Able at times to cry The note of pathos – but the stress is on the fact that only 'at times' is man human.

The Brothered-One, the Not-Alone Heavy personification, satirical of the brotherhood of man, the sticking together of the superior species to rule over the animal world.

For mother's fading hopes The whole verse is difficult because of the elliptical construction. It appears to mean that what his mother and nurse and father do is to repress his nature.

dead men never met His ancestors and their traditions.

mania ... desolation Fanaticism or failure.

The lion ... adder ... child Man and beast, nature and humanity must learn to live with each other, part of Auden's 'love' theme.

Musée des Beaux Arts

First published in 1939, this poem takes for its starting point the painting by Brueghel of *Icarus*, and the poet relates the extraordinary event depicted there to life, at the same time conveying the painter's own sense of perspective. There are two stanzas in the poem, the first easy and conversational in tone, perhaps deceptively casual, just as life is casual for some and significant for others. It is in two parts, almost as if the structure and divisions of a sonnet had been extended to the twenty-one lines found here. The first thirteen lines consist of a statement about the relative importance and unimportance of things occurring at the same time, and asserts that the classical painters have succeeded in capturing this. The final eight lines (almost equivalent to the sestet of a sonnet) qualify this by a consideration of Brueghel's painting, and just like a painting, these lines have a form, a shape, and are thus much more tightly written in terms of rhyme and rhythm than the preceding lines. This is typical of Auden, who can be both colloquial and sophisticatedly technical in the same poem, as we have seen. It is too an instance of his wry humour, his acceptance of what life is and his certainty that great painters have captured its quality and its perspective. There is a very effective variation in the length of line in the first part of the poem.

The Old Masters The acknowledged classical painters.

How, when the aged ... the miraculous birth Strong associations are present here with the three wise men and the birth of Christ, 'miraculous' because born of the Virgin Mary.

They never forgot The Old Masters.

martyrdom ... its innocent behind on a tree Notice that Auden is creating word pictures, and that these have the effect of giving his poem unity, for he is describing pictures in an art gallery, and thus connecting the visual with the verbal as a representation of life. The tone here is ironic, in the same way that Brueghel displays an ironic sense of perspective in his painting; 'innocent' is a transferred epithet which adds to the irony, since the horse itself is innocent although it carried the victim of the torturers.

Brueghel's *Icarus* The latter was the son of Daedalus. He flew too near the sun and his wax-fastened wings consequently melted. Pieter Brueghel (1525–69) was a celebrated Flemish painter.

the ploughman ... important failure Again the sense of perspective is evident, together with the irony. For the ploughman the death of an unknown man is not as important as the failure of his crops.

white legs ... green Water Simple, effective description, as clear-cut as the painting itself.

Sonnets from China

In the notes below, these are treated as a sequence. They constitute 'In Time of War', printed at the conclusion of *Journey to a War*, written by Auden and Isherwood about the Sino–Japanese War and published in 1939.

In the first Sonnet the octave and the sestet are clearly

divided, though the triplets of the sestet are run on into rhyming couplets. The sequence has been likened to Pope's *Essay on Man*. In the first section of Sonnet 1 the Creation is described in its natural evolutionary beginnings – each creature developing into the state and function natural to it. Then the sestet, with its divisions marked, records the arrival of man, with his conflicts (the leopard and the dove), his vulnerability, his emotions, his ideals (mistaken sometimes), and his love, which he chooses. Man shapes, nature is shaped; man makes his destiny, animals do not. Sonnet 2 begins after the Fall, with man's reaction to God's decree, the poet's tone conversational and modern (see line 3). Immediately he experiences change after the loss of innocence, with a different view and the realization of the necessity to adjust. But there is no return despite the coming of imagination and the need to make laws; the state of innocence, once lost, cannot be regained, and man must endure his suffering.

Sonnet 3 focuses on the use of language, the giving of names by which he makes 'connection', and from then on words 'breed' and language becomes the ruler and not the slave of man. The fourth Sonnet contrasts the primitive but noble savage way of life with the sophisticated life of man in the towns, and No. 5 represents the further development of man (again modern terms are satirically employed) as he expands into the cities and acquires all the authority of pedantic utterance and dislike of life. Sonnet 6 traces the portents of truth, both astrological and fortuitous – forecasting and chance – and traces too the intellectual pursuit of truth, then the side-tracking into mysticism and other 'arts', with the final realization of the appalling truth of truth – the reflection of 'every human weakness'. In No. 7 the focus switches to poetry, with the emphasis in the first part on the prophetic function of the poet which is ultimately displaced by the satirical mode – and this itself is perhaps further evidence of human weakness.

Sonnet 8 traces the evolution of the spiritual, the political, ideological and financial aspects of man's existence, ending with failure in the most important of all human qualities, love, for everything has grown so fast. The mythology of No. 9 appears to be classical, but there is certainly a strong suggestion of divine power and the reactions of man leading, one feels, to killing and corruption rather than love. The tenth Sonnet is really a summary of the evils of society, the traditions gone, the life of the imagination replaced by material concerns and economic necessity. Sonnet 11 opens with an invocation, a hope that man may create a just society, and then moves on to the contemplation of the actual war in China and its history. We thus see Auden's method, if we pause here for a moment; he has moved from the general to the specific by way of illustration.

To resume, No. 12 is given over to the description of typical war situations, but the idea that ideas must survive, that truth must be fought for, is inherent at the end of the poem, where the atrocious is given terrible weight by the reference to the two centres of atrocity – 'Nanking', 'Dachau'. Sonnet 13 looks at the ordinary soldier, his life and death, the irony taking in the 'writing up' of history, the soldier being compared to a comma. The fourteenth Sonnet is set in a military hospital, with the essential isolation given a considered stress, while No. 15 is an ironic account of the deliberations of the leaders whose decisions cost lives. Sonnet 16 describes the defeat of imperialism, of materialism, of those who bent others to their will. In No. 17 a bitter attack is launched on the way people are undermined by the crude appeals of Fascism which has 'pleased the dancers' by its triumphs of the year 'When Austria died'. The eighteenth Sonnet was to have been the final one of the sequence, a wish for the return of the beginning, for 'A taste of joy in an innocent mouth', though in face we are far removed from it. Despite the nature of the sestet, Auden recurs to the stoicism of Rilke in No. 19, and thus sounds an optimistic note – that there is some kind of hope in waiting and achieving. Sonnet 20 continues to centre on those who have gained fame or immortality in different ways. Then comes No. 21, the original dedicatory sonnet, to the great English novelist E. M. Forster, perhaps best remembered as the author of *A Passage to India*. The close reference to the novels underlines an attack on middle-class prejudices and standards typified by the characters named; by referring to Forster's 'insisting that the inner life can pay' Auden seems to be pinning man's hopes on spiritual integrity. It is difficult to see this poem as a conclusion, and one wonders if even here the ever-present Auden irony is merely closing an unpleasant chapter in man's history; with the Second World War scarcely a year away, this would not have been unlikely. The summaries given above, though necessarily brief, may be of help in understanding the outline of the sequence.

Sonnet 1

Bee took the politics i.e. the way of administration in its own community.

finned An unusual verbal usage.

hour of birth ... college Their learning was intuitive.

a leopard or a dove Fierce or mild. Auden goes on to enumerate in the next three lines the qualities of man.

Sonnet 2

the fruit i.e. the apple in the Garden of Eden.

The dogs ... The stream The loss of innocence involves non-communication with the simple things of life – nature.

the poet and the legislator The onset of imagination and the emergence of man-made laws means the complete loss of innocence and the impossibility of regaining it.

Sonnet 3

He, though, by naming The reference is to man and the fact that 'names' describe but are not identical with what is described.

He shook with hate ... Pined for a love i.e. the coming of irrational emotions which destroy man's balance.

And was oppressed i.e. man rules man, and his spirits too are oppressed by the weight of the world.

Sonnet 4

The mountains chose the mother A typical Auden emphasis – he means that man chose a mate from his immediate environment.

unnatural Note the force of the word, implying that man has grown away from nature.

Unhappy poets took him for the truth An ironic comment on the tendency of many poets to idealize the simple life.

Sonnet 5

about Law and Order The capitals underline the ironic tone, the heavy-handed way in which parents sometimes pronounce.

Sonnet 6

He watched the stars The beginning of the section which deals with approaches to the truth, or what appears to be the truth.

Truth The personification effectively conveys the importance of man's search, but leaves us with the abject ending of this sonnet which concludes with the reflection of 'every human weakness'.

Sonnet 7

He was Probably Homer or the poet.

The petty tremors i.e. he became subjective, diminished himself.

strophe One of the sections of a choral ode.

Sonnet 8

Equality Probably a reference to democracy.

set a paper spy i.e. the rule of paper money.

And lived expensively A reference to the industrial, materialistic society.

Sonnet 9

He looked ... the humble boy A reference to the myth of Jove and Ganymede.

Sonnet 10

giant's ... dragon ... kobold i.e. manifestations of evils and
fears in the past; the sonnet goes on to show that evil is *within* man
in any age. A kobold is a spirit.

the slot i.e. the dragon's lair.

The vanquished powers i.e. those of evil.

Sonnet 11

vegetal Of the nature of plants.

an engine i.e. power.

**The flower-like Hundred Families ... In the Eighteen
Provinces** This is a reference to Japanese imperialism.

Sonnet 12

like a monument Ironic, since monuments are often raised to
the dead.

a myriad faces/Ecstatic from one lie A reference to mass
hysteria, a common response to dictators like Hitler and
Mussolini.

Nanking. Dachau The first the official capital of the Chinese
loyalists, heavily bombed and devastated, the second the
notorious Nazi concentration camp.

Sonnet 13

Under a padded quilt he turned to ice i.e. died of exposure.

tidied into books Fine irony to indicate how divorced history is
from common humanity.

runeless A reference to the earliest alphabet used by the Anglo-
Saxons – a typical Auden coinage in this context to indicate the
primitive understanding of the Chinese soldier.

Might keep their upright carriage This parts deals with the
rape and degradation of Chinese women at the hands of the
Japanese.

Sonnet 14

like epochs Fine linking of man and time.

can become a foot Auden is referring to the loss of a limb which
becomes the centre of man's reaction or being.

Sonnet 15

waited for a verbal error Again the ironic appraisal of the reality.

Sonnet 16

disterred Archaic, meaning 'deprived of land or country'.

shadow-wife Fine, almost Anglo-Saxon coinage in emphasis – never to be forsaken, is always with them.

A native disapprove them with a stare ... Freedom's back This appears to refer to the defeat of imperialism.

Sonnet 17

the dancers best i.e. those moving to a certain pattern which, judging from the lines which precede this one, follow the forces of dictatorship.

Austria ... China Auden is working up to his indictment of appeasement, for Hitler took Austria without a struggle in 1938 while the militaristic aggression of the Japanese against the Chinese was ignored by the West.

Shanghai in flames The city and international centre was devastated by street fighting, raids and terrible scenes of carnage.

Teruel re-taken The capital of Teruel province in Spain, besieged by Government forces and taken in December 1937.

Partout/Il a de la joie Everywhere there's happiness (ironic).

Do you love me as I love you The classical statement of the policy of non-intervention – the answer is 'You don't, and therefore I won't help you'.

Sonnet 18

A warm nude age i.e. the innocence of Eden.

Sonnet 19

pandemic Disease prevalent over the whole of a country or the world.

Until in Muzot The reference is to the German poet Rainer Maria Rilke 1875–1926, who was a great influence on Auden. There is a moving quality here about his 'ivory tower' life in Muzot (Switzerland) where he laboured to complete his *Duino Elegies*.

Sonnet 20

genus Species, race, class.

kennel Mean dwelling.

incognito i.e. unnamed.

in our blood/If we allow them i.e. they can be a positive life in us if we wish it – this is a reference to the past, our predecessors.

Sonnet 21

E. M. Forster (1879–1970) The celebrated novelist.

Italy and King's Two of Forster's early novels have Italian settings in which the contrast with English life is emphasized: *Where Angels Fear to Tread* (1905) and *A Room With A View* (1908). He was an honorary fellow of King's College, Cambridge from 1946 until his death.

Truth ... bombs discuss Heavy irony at the expense of military aggression.

the inner life i.e. spiritual, moral, intellectual.

like the telephone Auden is adept at noticing, and including, the reflexes of the modern pace of life.

Lucy A character riddled with middle-class standards in *A Room With A View*.

Turton Representative of the British Raj attitude in *A Passage to India*.

Philip In *Where Angels Fear to Tread*, he appears to be enlightened but isn't, though he does experience a moment of truth.

reason is denied and love ignored Note the antithetical balance of this.

Miss Avery In Chapter 41 of *Howard's End* (1920) Charles Wilcox strikes Leonard Bast with a sword and kills him. Just after this the chapter ends with the words ' "Yes, murder's enough," said Miss Avery, coming out of the house with the sword.'

In memory of W. B. Yeats

This was published in March 1939, and is divided into three parts; the first is in heavy elegiacs as befits the subject, with a refrain in verses one and five, while the second contemplates the fact that 'poetry makes nothing happen' and the third, with a kind of Blakeian lyricism ('Tiger, Tiger') considers the 'Intellectual disgrace' of the time and urges the elevating function of the poet. This is bald summary and does scant justice to the technical variety displayed within the poem, for Auden moves from the specific (Yeats's death) to the general, equating man with the cities 'dying' at the hands of the dictator; from thence he moves on to look at poetry, and then to the function of the poet in evil times.

W. B. Yeats (1856–1939) The great Irish poet and thinker whose verse is even more esoteric than Auden's, and with whom Auden felt a strong affinity.

disfigured the public statues Note the emphasis on the outer cold and the implication that Yeats in death is a statue.

the mouth of the dying day Again, nature equated with man, the whole phrase approximating to the taking of the temperature of the dying poet.

The wolves ran on ... The peasant river References which embrace Ireland and perhaps the mythology of Yeats's own poems.

The death of the poet was kept from his poems The poet may be dead and forgotten – his poems live on.

The provinces ... squares ... current of his feeling A fine evocation which compares man to a country, and there is a strong note of the threats and menace of the thirties – the invasions by the dictators – behind it.

another kind of wood i.e. not that of nature, but the coffin.

a foreign code of conscience Perhaps that of God.

The words of a dead man ... guts of the living i.e. what he wrote meant one thing to him, but what it means to the living man now reading it may be different.

the Bourse Money-market, here the Paris stock-exchange.

the cell of himself Refers to the individual 'trapped' within his own body, but by association makes one think of the poet 'trapped' in the coffin.

You were silly Yeats was eccentric, frequently wayward and unpredictable.

The parish of rich women A reference to Yeats's patrons, foremost among them being his life-long friend Lady Gregory.

Mad Ireland A reference to the troubles and conflicts, more particularly the Easter rising of 1916, which Yeats commemorated in a poem with the moving refrain 'A terrible beauty is born'.

For poetry makes nothing happen Perhaps not, but the last verse of the whole poem envisages the function of the poet in idealistic, loving terms.

a mouth i.e. because poetry speaks.

Earth This section, though reminiscent of Blake, has other echoes, particularly of Shelley and Gray's *Elegy*. The lightness of tone is to be equated with the optimistic ideal – the greatness of Yeats's poetry, his function as a singer and teacher, may be found again by other poets.

dogs of Europe i.e. the dictators.

To the bottom of the night An echo here of Blake's 'Tiger, tiger, burning bright/In the forests of the night'.

unconstraining An important word, in view of the cell and coffin imagery earlier.

a vineyard of the curse Strongly Biblical in association.

deserts ... fountain ... prison ... free Note how effectively Auden is using contrast to underline the need for imaginative and spiritual inspiration.

Domesday song

This was published in 1941, and consists of four short, six-line verses which examine the inevitability of time, the death which comes to the beautiful flower (orchid), the swan (beauty) and Caesar (man). Verse two traces the degradation wrought by time, while birth and death are the focus of verse three, with man, as we have seen earlier, the agent of death in the animal world. There is no escape from the inexorability of time, and the poem ends with a nursery rhyme parody and a tongue-twister which perhaps parallels the twisted nature of the life which ends.

one common box i.e. death (for man, the coffin).

Prophets ... profit Deliberate punning to show the shortness of life and success – prophecy becomes fact (or otherwise) and profit soon disappears.

Persona grata An acceptable person.

jackass language i.e. braying, nonsense, indicating a change of style or fashion in speaking or writing which shocks others.

clocks ... Index finger i.e. the passing of time, the note that it is time to go to bed.

fox ... gun The hunting that leads to death.

made the docks i.e. escaped.

Round the rampant The parody conveys the fact that we move in a circle, that we cannot escape, that we are all for judgement, hence the title of the poem.

If I could tell You

This, despite the repetition and the epigrammatic tone, is again concerned with the inevitability of life, and appears to be a parody of a popular song in which cynicism replaces the commercially-successful cliché. It is written in the form of a villanelle, and keeps to that structure, though Auden manages to introduce his own individual imagery, here of lions, brooks and soldiers, thus giving to the monotony of facts his own unusual or rather unexpected associations. The villanelle has 19 lines, consisting of 15 in triplets with alternate lines rhyming, and concluding with a quatrain which is the climax of the repetition and the monotony of word-play.

The vision i.e. the dream, which lasts but a moment.

lions ... brooks ... soldiers A typical Auden reversal, a fantasy.

Atlantis

According to Plato, an ideal commonwealth existed in Atlantis, a legendary island in the Atlantic ocean. Here the seven verses of twelve lines each describe the search for truth. The imagery is geographical in the first verse, with the colloquial ('The Boys') also figuring prominently. The second verse is in praise of intellectual humanism (as in the Ionia of the past), the third deals with the Dionysiac and orgiastic yielding in Thrace, the fourth is given up to the temptations of the flesh as typified in Carthage or Corinth. Thus far this 'quest' has proved to have many temptations, attractions and lures which lead one from what is essentially spiritual. But the next verse underlines this movement towards the spiritual, with the traveller sustained, according to the poet, by the memory of the 'noble dead'. The imagery now is that of ascent, of mountaineering (remember that Auden's brother was a famous mountaineer), with the sight of fulfilment but not the complete experience of it. Thus the 'quest' is not only for spiritual completeness but perhaps also for artistic expression, creation, as well. The echoes in the last verse are pagan, but the ending may be summarized as meaning that the journey in pursuit of truth or art is a blessing in itself.

Ship of Fools Written in German in 1494, the story tells of the various classes of fools being deported from their own country to a land of fools.

The Boys ... Hard liquor i.e. you must be prepared to conform, to become one of the ordinary sinners if you are to reach your goal.

Ionia Thin strip of land on the West Coast of Asia Minor colonized by the Greeks.

Thrace Vast tract of country bounded on the north by the Danube.

conch Shell of a mollusc, perhaps used as a trumpet.

Carthage In ancient times, city on the North coast of Africa, head of the great Phoenician commercial empire.

Corinth The great Greek city one and a half miles south of the isthmus which connects Peloponnesus with central Greece.

This is Atlantis, dearie Notice the injection of the modern colloquial sordidness of the prostitute's language.

Counterfeit Atlantis The ironic aside – all substitutes for the
perfect life.

Tundras Barren regions with frozen subsoil.

Dialectic i.e. testing the truth by questioning or discussion.

col A depression in the mountain chain.

household gods i.e. essentials of home life (which urge you not
to go).

Hermes In Greek mythology the son of Zeus. He became his
father's messenger, and the patron of merchants and travellers.

the four dwarf Kabiri The Kabeiroi were metal-worshipping
dwarfs, worshipped as gods in the Hellenic mythology.

the Ancient of Days i.e. God ('Most blessed, most glorious,/The
ancient of days/Almighty victorious/Thy great name we praise'),
according to the hymn.

The fall of Rome

First published in 1947, this poem consists of seven quatrains,
with the second and third lines forming a couplet enclosed by
the 'a' rhymes. The atmosphere is nightmarish, visual, the
representation of the decline of society. In fact there is a
constant interaction between the decadence of the present and
that of the past, a favourite Auden device, with the sensual
and the commonplace used to counterbalance each other. The
last two verses focus on nature, the first indicating the
spread of disease and corruption, while the second expresses
its beauty and majesty in obvious contrast to the decline of
civilization.

Fantastic grow the evening gowns Note the immediate
contrast with nature, for this is the artificial growth in decadence.

Fisc The treasury of Ancient Rome.

Private rites Another underlining of the moral decay.

literati Men of letters, the learned class.

Cerebrotonic Cato Cato the Younger (95–46 BC) who fortified
himself by the Stoic philosophy and ultimately stabbed himself to
death rather than fall into the hands of Caesar.

muscle-bound Marines A deliberate updating, to make one
think of modern times.

Caesar's double-bed ... I DO NOT LIKE MY WORK
Contrast between the mighty and the commonplace, but both
underline the lack of moral fibre, the 'fall' of standards.

A walk after dark

Eight short, six-lined verses in which the poet contemplates
the night sky and measures his own life (and the life of man)
in relation to it. There is the usual subtlety of reference in
the first verse, but this gives way to the reminiscence of
adolescence in the second, with its do's and don't's of that
time. The third verse, stressing his own middle-aged state,
takes comfort from the fact that the stars at least are still
there – they are middle-aged too by his own measure! Verse
four continues the theme, with some note of the 'red pre-
Cambrian light', comparing the changes in civilizations to
those in man; the fifth verse probes the emotional tendencies
of the 'young and the rich', while the sixth turns to the
inevitability of human suffering. It stresses the idea that even
at this moment we may be on the edge of some significant
change. The final verse returns to the contemplation of the
night, with its own unconscious permanence, as distinct from
the changes which await both individuals and nations. The
tone throughout is quiet, with something of the wisdom of
stored experience, effectively establishing the continuity of life,
the cosmic relationship, the links of present and past.

The clockwork spectacle i.e. because of its regularity.
Eighteenth-century way A reference to man's scientific
discoveries at the time, and to the age of rational appraisal.
points i.e. by which man steers (navigation as well as his way
through life, for they measure the passing of time).
an Old People's Home Typical sudden change of emphasis –
the image carries a 'community' association which deepens the
relationship between man and the night.

pre-Cambrian light A reference to the period in which marine and animal life were first manifested.

The stoic manner i.e. control of the passions and indifference to pleasure and pain; the stoics were founded as a 'school' of philosophy at Athens by Zeno in 308 BC.

lacrimae rerum Latin, the tears of things. From Vergil's Aeneid I line 462.

post-diluvian i.e. after the Flood.

The quest

This begins as a sonnet sequence, like the *Sonnets from China*, but variants occur within it. Both Fuller and Spears append the following quotation from Auden to the sequence:

The theme of the Quest occurs in fairy tales, legends like the Golden Fleece and the Holy Grail, boys' adventure stories and detective novels. These poems are reflections upon certain features common to them all. The 'He' and 'They' referred to should be regarded as both objective and subjective.

This is *essential* to any student reading the poems, for the reverberations of the language, as might be expected, are esoteric, often referring to one of the *genres* named above. The first Sonnet deals with the subconscious, 'our future', what life holds in store for us, our fears of the past, and our escapes into it, like Alice's. Verbal interpretation cannot do justice to the Freudian implications of the verse, and the student must respond to the associations of the poems rather than being intent on a detailed, line-by-line interpretation, to which Auden's writing rarely lends itself. The second Sonnet indicates the preparations for setting out on the journey, the search for the unknown, with the emphasis on the 'modern' equipment needed – instruments, a watch, drugs – while the explorer-cum-missionary images of the octave provide a typical Auden focus. The sestet indicates the futility of the preparations, since man is in his 'situation': hence he cannot escape from it. The third Sonnet opens with strong legendary associations, with the competition, the time taken to complete the test, the year and a day associated with, for example, the Middle English poem of *Sir Gawain and the Green Knight*. This is rather longer than the preceding sections, but the fourth reverts to the sonnet form. From the suburb to the meadows, the castle, the bridges, the thickets, the whole description shows man within reach of God, yet desolate, unable to avail himself of the completeness he desires, unable to act positively. Sonnet 5 describes his arrival in the city, the reduction of the individual by the experience and the obvious loss of individual identity which ensues. The sixth Sonnet describes the yielding to the lure of being popular, the consequent spoiling of self, the inability to accept the reality of life, the truths which are eternal. The seventh represents the rejection of life, the expression of disgust, the temptation towards suicide. The eighth traces the movement away from others to the complete dedication to self, and yet with a kind of subconscious awareness that such concern with self is inherently evil. The ninth Sonnet describes through the symbol of the tower (cf. Yeats) the withdrawal from experience with its divine associations, but considers that, at the same time, earthly needs may become insistent. The tenth uses the language of legend to define various failures in the search for the truth, while the eleventh posits a particular kind of failure, the failure of the child through the ambition of the parents. Self-knowledge comes at the end of the sestet and with it, of course, the fear of failure. The twelfth Sonnet recounts the rejection of one who wished to become a martyr (a soldier), was turned down, and consequently takes a place 'among the tempters', the thirteenth lists several categories of failure as well, but stresses their usefulness to others. The fourteenth is an unusual Sonnet, the lines being in couplets and of a much longer, conversationally rhythmic tone. This is an outline of the negative approaches which, of course, can never reach the truth. The fifteenth reinforces this, for in fact those who achieve anything are merely those who are fortunate by chance. The sixteenth is an ironic description of the hero, the routine conscientious worker and parrier of questions who merely takes the trouble to do what he has to do with humility, and whose heroic qualities are therefore not evident. The seventeenth underlines the qualities of diplomacy and non-commitment of those who are not heroes, the majority of people incapable of going beyond 'convention'. The eighteenth represents the denials of the flesh – another retreat from life into asceticism – which is recorded in art and is supposed to provide fertility for others, though in itself is arid. The nineteenth is another unusual Sonnet, shorter-lined, showing that no matter who or what a person is, he must receive the same treatment as others, since all are un-aware of what is to follow. The final Sonnet has a strong emphasis on love. This is another allegorical poem dealing with man's journey through life; the verbal difficulties and ambiguities are an established part of Auden's method, and perhaps reflect the difficulties of the 'quest'. There are various levels of interpretation – the quest can be for knowledge, artistic fulfilment, happiness, the spiritual, the quest for the 'real self' of each individual.

Sonnet 1

Out of it Spears suggests the 'it' is the threshold between the conscious mind and the unconscious.

Her Majesty Strong associations here with Lewis Carroll's *Alice in Wonderland*.

A red-nosed Fool Note the distorted effect of the 'dream'.

missionary grin ... foaming inundation Note the effect of the contrast – the individual power and the power of nature.

Simply by being tiny Alice, we remember, grew too large for the 'wonderland' she had entered by drinking from the bottle. The passage underlines our subconscious frustrations.

Sonnet 2

Drugs to move the bowels or the heart The preparation is almost for a mountaineering expedition, a typical Auden image. Note the antithetical irony in this phrase.

And coloured beads i.e. with which to bribe 'savages' – but remember that the imagery is allegorical.

One should not i.e. one must avoid doing what is superfluous, not needed because already provided.

Sonnet 3

The journey that should take no time at all i.e. because we are confident of achieving it. Again, an ironic comment.

Sonnet 4

Greater Hallows Saints' relics.

To be his father's house and speak his mother tongue This appears to mean that the invitation to return to innocence is there.

Sonnet 5

being nobody ... watched the country kids The implication is that all are seduced by the town into losing identity, and those thus corrupted delight in the corruption of those who arrive.

Sonnet 6

Roman food He uses his imagination to transform his hunger into illusory feasts.

flattered duchess Exaggerated term for 'lover'.

to his tall belief i.e. the world of imagination he had made for himself, rather than the reality of living.

Sonnet 7

(Remember that the 'He' is both objective and subjective according to Auden's definition).

And plunged i.e. suicide.

Sonnet 8

the Devil's Waltz i.e. temptation.

someone with his own distorted features i.e. himself, and
here it represents a recognition of his own selfishness and self-
indulgence.

Sonnet 9

a virgin made/Her maidenhead Danae was imprisoned by her
father in a tower, but was ravished by Jove.

natural climate . . . Beware of Magic The contrast underlines
the theme of the sonnet – the withdrawal from life into private
and esoteric ritual (or its equivalent) as distinct from taking part
in everyday life.

Sonnet 10

virginity . . . unicorn The latter is the fabulous animal who is
the emblem of female chastity in Christian art.

desert lions . . . ogre and were turned to stone
Representations of those who failed – again the connections with
legends and fairy stories is obvious.

Sonnet 11

Average Man The whole verse echoes this – those who are
ordinary cannot achieve the extraordinary.

Sonnet 12

Those whose request to suffer i.e. volunteering to serve and
being turned down, not being allowed to be a 'hero'.

His pacing manias His obsessions (towards grandeur).

Sonnet 13

By standing stones All things have their uses, as the rest of this
verse demonstrates.

Sonnet 14

of the Way i.e. towards the fulfilment, on whatever level or levels
we take it.

the old horse i.e. the odds must be stacked against him, and – as
the next lines imply – he must be clean-living.

the chapel in the rock Echoes of T. S. Eliot's *The Waste Land*
and the search for the *Holy Grail*.

the Triple Rainbow Fuller points out that the reference comes from Doughty's *Arabia Deserta*, 'the peace in heaven after the battle of the elements'.

the Astral Clock Probably regulated by sidereal time.

Sonnet 15

cryptogram i.e. written in cipher. Auden is now well into the detective, mystery novel *genre* here, as the other references show.

Sphinx The fabulous animal, invention of the Egyptians, which tormented travellers by asking for the answer to a riddle.

I won the Queen because my hair was red i.e. by chance, good fortune.

in Grace i.e. in religion.

Sonnet 16

He parried This sonnet deals with the real hero – Fuller suggests that T. E. Lawrence (Lawrence of Arabia) may have been in Auden's mind here.

Sonnet 17

The crowd clung all the closer i.e. finding their security in that.

Absconded God i.e. who has left them because of what they are – an enigmatic way of saying that they themselves have deserted the Christian or good way of life.

Sonnet 18

The Negative Way i.e. the journey towards ascetisicm. The aridity of it and what it leads to is described in the next few lines.

They seeded out These next few lines describe the legends associated with these desert fathers (i.e. the gift of fertility for others) and their representation in art.

Sonnet 19

apperception The mind's perception of itself.

vectors of their interest Presumably the lines, which have a fixed length and direction but no fixed position.

Sonnet 20

This was originally titled 'The Garden', hence the strong associations with innocence.

seven earnest sins i.e. sins which will come later – children
  merely play at them.
tall conditions i.e. those who impose conditions on them – their
  masters or controllers.
Another's moment of consent i.e. physical love.
Roses have flung their glory A word-picture of simple rustic
  beauty as a compensation for 'desolation'.
their centre of volition shifted i.e. what they lived by had
  changed.

from The sea and the mirror
II The supporting cast *sotto voce*

This series of dramatic continuations, in a variety of verse forms, imaginatively follows the end of Shakespeare's *The Tempest*, (the sub-title of the sequence is *A Commentary on Shakespeare's The Tempest*), and it is rightly called by Spears 'a definition and exploration of the relations between the Mirror of Art and the Sea of Life or Reality'. Auden's variety of styles is interspersed, as in Shakespeare's play, with songs. Spears further categorizes the *genre* as 'closet drama', and this again appropriately indicates its limitations. Prior to the extracts printed here, this 'continuation' of *The Tempest* has an address from the Stage Manager, then the prompter, the packing up of Prospero and his goodbye to Ariel, while this in turn is followed by the cast speaking *sotto voce* as we see here. The influence of the experiences in the play are upon them, but they are in the process of moving out into life. The final speaker is Caliban, given (ironically in view of his 'bestial' role in *The Tempest*) easily the most to say, and he does this in the language – and at the length – of Henry James. Before reading this selection, and this commentary on it, the student must acquaint himself with the plot of *The Tempest* and the *original* functions in that play of the characters who speak here. All the extracts are from this second section with Antonio, the usurping villain of *The Tempest* providing his own linking commentary on what is said. He is still the representative of evil, and is the reverse of all that has occurred to the other characters. He puts the view that Prospero's 'art' is still operating, that everything is illusory, and maintains his own immunity to Prospero's power – thus, by inference, refusing to let Prospero forsake it. This is his revenge for Prospero's triumph in the play, and after each character has spoken Antonio mutters his comments, thus ensuring his own dramatic dominance. As will be seen, each character has his say – Ferdinand in love for Miranda, Stephano in love for his stomach – and Gonzalo (a noble if pedantic character in the play), after defining his own role in the past action, now feels that he can express the will of God. Adrian and Francisco, two courtiers, comment in two lines on the reality behind appearance, and then Alonso, King of Naples, whose son Ferdinand is restored to him by Prospero, gives that son instructions on the nobility of his office, counsels him against pride, urges him to steer a middle and just way. Here the third verse centres on betrayal and ridicule (both themes in *The Tempest*); the fourth describes the temptations which lure princes from the way of honour and rectitude, while the fifth warns against the delusory effects of happiness and grandeur, for that is when fate always strikes. The sixth re-iterates the prerequisites of the middle way, and the seventh continues the arguments for moderation and temperance. The eighth shows that this is in the form of a letter to Ferdinand which is to be read after Alonso's death. The song of the master and the boatswain is a subtle reworking with imaginative variants of Stephano's song in *The Tempest* (Act II, Scene 2), having a licentious tone which is underpinned by a pathetic stress on loneliness.

Antonio

As all the pigs have turned back into men A reference to
  Prospero's magic – and further back still to the enchantress Circe,
  who detained Ulysses and his men by turning them into pigs.

Two heads i.e. of Ferdinand and Miranda, the lovers.

the lean/Fool Trinculo.

dear old butler Stephano, ironically described, since he is often
  'drunken'.

What a lot a little music can do Music is one aspect of
  Prospero's art, and is lyrically referred to by Caliban.

while I stand outside/Your circle Antonio is arguing that if he
  resists Prospero's art, Prospero will not be able to forsake it.

occluded Enclosed, shut off, obstructed.

all is partial This occurs in the song, variants of which are sung
  by Antonio in commentary; here the epigrammatic terseness
  reflects the will of Antonio.

Your need to love Heavy irony at the expense of Prospero.

Ferdinand

Flesh, fair Note that Ferdinand, as befits a lover, speaks in
  simple single-word effects which define his beloved.

Dear Other Miranda.

One bed is empty Note that Antonio's comment again
  underlines his *singleness* – of purpose – and thus resistance to what
  Prospero has done, ensuring that what has affected others will not
  affect him.

Stephano

A lost thing looks for a lost name His search for being, for
  identity, and a reference surely to his being so often drunk that he
  doesn't know who he is.

a vulgar pooh i.e. indicative of contempt.

One glass is untouched i.e. Antonio is determined not to be
  'under the influence' of Prospero.

Gonzalo

welkin Sky.

ambient Surrounding.

rusting flesh i.e. old age.

locus Exact place.

Adrian and Francisco

good little sunbeams ... madly ungay Fuller rightly refers to this as 'a rather camp couplet'.

Alonso

the sand ... Sofa or mutilated statue Note the vividness of the word picture, symbolic of decay.

The scorpion i.e. which can sting, thus symbolic of action against the throne.

the Shark and the octopus Symbols of murder or assassination.

subscription/Concerts i.e. where nothing is provided.

the sea in which ... or the desert the contrast is between sensual life and the life of self-denial, but the word pictures which convey it are particularly vivid.

efreet Evil spirit, demon.

Cupolas Rounded domes forming roofs.

Ecbatana The capital of ancient Media, favourite summer residence of the Kings of Persia.

fire and ice i.e the extremes, here of action.

The spring in the desert ... Island in the sea i.e. the ideal balance between the flesh and the spirit which the King must achieve.

Music strike and seen the statue move He is referring to Prospero's art, but of course the lines echo *The Winter's Tale* (Act V, Scene 3) where Paulina's invocation to 'Music' has the statue of Hermione coming to life.

Master and Boatswain

The homeless played ... i.e. the sailors.

I was not looking for a cage i.e. I was not going to be trapped (into marriage).

The nightingales are sobbing in A direct echo of T. S. Eliot's *Sweeney Among the Nightingales*, but there the nightingales (prostitutes) are singing.

Sebastian

Prudence flirted with a naked sword A reference to the conspiracy to kill Alonso.

the white bull Presumably symbolic of Antonio's bravery as distinct from the previous cowardice of Sebastian.

Trinculo

A terror shakes my tree ... This verse shows his loneliness and fear of life.

The paradox Antonio i.e. He will be celebrating his own immunity from Prospero.

Miranda

Note that this is another villanelle.

the Black Man ... The Witch ... the Ancient Perhaps connected with Caliban and his mother Sycorax (who was a witch), but notice that the first runs away, the second dissolves, and the 'Ancient' prays – all is changed for good.

as children in a circle dancing Symbolic of innocence and purity, completeness.

My Dear One Notice that this is the refrain, and thus symbolic of a lyrical expression of love.

Dances for Death alone i.e. the death, perhaps, of Prospero's art.

In praise of limestone

This was published in 1948, and is a wonderful invocation to landscape, in blank verse lines of sonorous, serious rhythm as befits contemplation and the associations set up by contemplation. The poem is in worship of nature, of the great earth-mother who provides, and of man's ability to control and organize what is provided in a given area, for example stone, water, used by man in various ways. This is the burthen of the first part; in the second man is seen against the foreground of this nature, but is contrasted with sophisticated man and political intrigue, to indicate one emphasis, while the infinite corruptibility of man in society is set against the acceptance of man in nature. The attractions of other kinds of landscape are explored, modified by man to his sophisticated use, and there is some examination of the lure of the sea. The poem then becomes more intimate in tone, with the poet reflecting on the landscape again, its history, its function in the modern world; he records the beauty that can be fashioned from it, while from the poet's point of view it is redolent of love, of associations which have a permanent place in the heart. There is an elegiac note throughout, but both the control and the range of imaginative reference are magnificent.

with a chuckle An endearing brief personification.

weathered outcrop Emerging of rock, vein, stratum at surface.

To receive more attention Auden is really here tracing the essentially competitive spirit of man – to achieve more than his contemporaries – and to be seen to be achieving more.

gennels Long, narrow passages.

but never, thank God, in step Auden is here distinguishing between what is natural and what is regimented, doubtless with a backward look at the dictatorships of Hitler and Mussolini.

a clever line ... a good lay Deluded by smart talk or ideas or sexual invitation.

the lattice-work of a nomad's comb A superb image to convey man's freedom from society and convention against the landscape.

'Come!' cried the granite wastes Note that the three areas 'speak' with their particular 'invitations'.

his mind Puzzle Perhaps 'puzzling out', seeking to put things in a new way.

antimythological myth Probably, because the statues support the myth.

gamins Street arabs, boys.

Innocent athletes i.e. representations, statues perhaps of the Olympics.

Fleet visit

Published in 1952, on the face of it it is a slight poem, five verses of six short lines, but the mention of the 'hollow ships' immediately sets up classical associations (the Greeks laying siege to Troy). The contemporary context is that of a NATO exercise showing that America is strong and prepared to defend (for example, Europe) some seven years after the end of the Second World War. The tone is ironic, light, conversational, the focus being on the cost of the ships and the admiration of their beauty as they stand in the harbour, for 'Their structures are humane'. The men are forgotten in the contemplation of the 'pattern and line'.

hollow ships Associated with the Greeks.
comic strips i.e. picture cartoons, here indicating lack of any real cultural interest or level.
Troys A reference to the Greek siege of Troy described by Homer in the *Iliad*. The Greeks finally destroyed the city.
because ... just-in-case Fine colloquial balance here conveying the uncertainty of post-war peace.
junk i.e. cheap rubbish.
the Social Beast i.e. the consumer society, with Auden being ironic through the personification.
Of the billions Despite the 'line' Auden is obviously still being ironic.

The shield of Achilles

Connected to the previous poem in that we are still in the post-war era, this poem has even stronger associations with the *Iliad*. The reader is advised to look closely at Book 18, where Thetis comforts Achilles for the death of Patroclus, and Vulcan, at her behest, forges a suit of armour and a splendid shield for Achilles. Again the focus is on the post-war world, with the shield reflecting aspects of a degraded rather than a re-organized or ordered way of life. The first verse describes the ideal which might have been, while the second describes the totalitarian reality – perhaps an indication that Nazism has been replaced by another kind of threat. Whereas the first verse is lyrically poetic, verse two descends into conversational flatness, equivalent to the 'flat' definition of reality. The third verse maintains the tone and is symbolic of factual and spiritual death at the whim of dictatorship. The fourth returns to the lyrical in tone and form as befits the hope of things spiritual, but the fifth approximates to a kind of concentration-camp updating of the crucifixion, the contemporary and the past thus linked in terms of injustice. The apathy of the mass of onlookers is described in the sixth, while the seventh, reverting to the pagan associations of the Olympic games, of joy in competitive endeavour, gives way in the eighth to the sordid reality of everyday life, a world of violence and rape. In the final verse the poet reverts to Thetis, but again with the omniscient irony of the contemporary world present in his innuendo.

shining metal i.e. the shield.

like lead Note that the description forecasts what is to come.

a million boots An immediate suggestion of Nazism or perhaps Communism.

Out of the air a voice God and God-like associations, but the idea of the mass radio broadcast is present.

Libation Drink offering to a god.

As three pale figures The echo of the crucifixion, Christ and the two thieves.

hope for help Note the word-play and the running alliteration.

And died as man before their bodies died i.e. they lost all individuality and purpose, and independence.

Hephaestos Vulcan The crippled armourer of the gods.

Thetis Wife to Peleus, mother of Achilles, and gifted with prophetic insight.

Iron-hearted ... Who would not live long Note that the contrast is immediately effective and applicable to those living in an uncertain world which has so much threat of death in it.

The Sabbath

This poem was published in 1959, and consists of seven quatrains, each approximating to one of the days of creation; the tone is casual, conversational and ironic, the direct source being Genesis, with the animals apparently glad to be free of man. Later the 'rifle's ringing crack' will establish man's lordship over them. The final verse underlines the fact that man was created in God's image.

the Seventh Day of Creation i.e. when God rested.

Herbivore i.e. living on grass and greenstuff.

Ruins and metallic rubbish Auden has the fascinating habit of updating into modern time, so that man and his untidy and wasteful nature is seen in modern terms.

His Impudence A grandiose way of describing man.

Arcadia A pagan reference (perhaps to underline the 'pagan' action). Arcadia was the pastoral tableland which was the home of Artemis and Pan.

More god-like i.e. made in the image of God, and with the power of reason.

First things first

This was published in 1957, and consists of five verses of six lines each, written in conversational and moving blank verse. It describes waking up in a storm, trying to make 'love-speech' from the noise of the elements, and at the same time it sets the memory in motion, recalling with that peculiar nostalgia and the intensity of loneliness a particular moment spent with the loved one. Finally, he sleeps again, realizing that when he wakes up the storm will have left the *facts* of its achievement (water in the cistern for example) rather than the love thoughts it gave rise to. This is a beautiful and touching poem, made poignant through the idea 'I lay in the arms of my own warmth'.

airy vowels ... watery consonants The storm is being dignified by such a reference, allowing it its own language.

Kenning Recognizing.

both real and imaginary monsters i.e. the beasts outside (in the storm) and the creatures of the imagination.

green ... pure blue A reference to the effects of the lightning.

As the stare of any rose A fine indication of the permanence of a moment in time.

all cultured Texans do i.e. a satirical remark at the expense of those who seek out 'culture' wherever they go.

fleeced by their guides i.e. robbed, and given false information.

Hegelian Bishops Presumably a reference to those who followed the philosophy of Hegel (1770–1831).

a leonine summer One that is golden, like the colour of the lion.

The old man's road

Published in 1956 this, according to Fuller, is the road of 'spiritual self-discovery', and the couplets are separated out into verses. The theme is that this self-discovery by-passes the traditional religions ('God's Vicar', for example) and keeps close to nature. It is thus another search or quest poem, here for the innocence, the purity, of the spiritual being. Freedom is essential ('No life ... That sticks to this course can be made captive') and history too is ignored.

the Great Schism Division, particularly of churches and faiths.

God's Vicar The Pope.

God's Ape Presumably, man, (or even the disestablished churches(?)).

The Old Man's Road i.e. that which leads to spiritual self-discovery.

cosmological myth Based on the science of the universe.

hill-top rings i.e. signifying burial-places.

Lovers' Lanes Auden is using his familiar geographical-cum-travel imagery to define the spiritual quest with its twists and turns.

Theocrat Ruler believing in government by God.

Apotropaically Turning away.

coleopterist Beetle hunter or collector.

Friday's child

Published in 1958, twelve quatrains on the theme of God giving man freedom of choice, a freedom which man has never grasped in terms of its implications. There is an obvious connection throughout with the proverbial rhyme about Friday's child, and the associations are equally obvious with Christ and Good Friday as well as with Bonhoeffer. The final verses revert to the Cross (or martyrdom) which man is free to interpret.

Dietrich Bonhoeffer (1906–45) A theologian who resisted Hitler and was arrested and tried – and hanged – for complicity in plots against him.

He told us i.e. God.

children as we were i.e. in Eden.

The bigger bangs A reference to atomic war.

Adam ... Acts of God i.e. Man will behave as if he were God – again a reference to the abuse of this by the dictators.

self-observed observing The implication is that the egoist's awareness is circumscribed, limited.

Unopened to the sender i.e. No matter what we do, we cannot discover the truth about God.

conscious unbelievers ... Judgement Day A reference to our superstitious fear that we shall be punished for our sins.

Bucolics

All seven are printed here, and Fuller notes that they were written before December 1953. The word 'bucolics' means 'pastoral poems', and here each is treated separately.

Section 1: *Winds*
The first verse of this poem (the first two are regular, the third twice the length, all in blank verse with some assonance and consonance) deals with the breath of life from God ('holy insufflation'). The appraisal takes in the idea that God might

have done better to breathe this positive form of life into another creature rather than 'bubble-brained' man. The second verse turns to winds as 'weather' and develops into a satirical look at weather as a habit (barometers, rain-gauge) for suburban man. The rest of the poem is really a casual invocation to the 'Goddess of winds' to provide him, the poet, with the inspiration to write. The final line virtually defines the areas of his choice – 'Earth, Sky, a few dear names'.

First Dad i.e. Adam.

boneless Fine word ironically included in the personification.

Metropolis The city (according to Fuller, the Fallen City).

Pliocene Of the newest division of Tertiary formation (a geological term).

teleost A group of bony fishes, including most living species.

arthropod Insect, spider.

I am loved, therefore I am A parody of Descartes 'I think therefore I am'.

the lion ... the kid Isaiah 11, 6.

Authentic City Presumably the city, true city, of today.

brigs Archaic for bridges.

paterfamilias The father of the family.

marram grass A shore grass that binds sand.

susurration Whispering, rustling.

anamnesis Recollection (perhaps of a previous existence).

Section 2: *Woods*

First published in 1952, these nine verses of iambic lines each consist effectively of a quatrain followed by a couplet. The first deals with the primitive woods so beloved of certain artists, the second with their being owned by squires and the crown and the church, while the third considers woods as conducive to seductions. The fourth looks at them as venues for picnics, the fifth for peace and relaxation. The sixth further stresses the noises of nature, the seventh specifically of leaves falling and 'water noise'. In the eighth Auden considers that 'well-kempt' woods reveal something of a 'country soul', and the ninth underlines this by indicating that the decline of a society begins with its cutting down of trees, concluding with the line 'A culture is no better than its woods'.

Piero di Cosimo (1462–1521) Florentine painter.

a stocks Timber frame with holds for feet, hands and head, used as a form of punishment.

most unsocial fires i.e. ritual, secret rites.

Crown and Mitre i.e. The King and the Church.

licence of the grove i.e. evil behaviour in the woods.

round the deed i.e. of seduction.

lower-ordersy the Gang How common everyone looks (in a snapshot).

By those vast lives Perhaps those depicted in art.

Bridle Rein in, that is curb its (other) interests.

philologist One who is interested in the science of language.

the matter of his field i.e. from which language (names) came.

Pan's green father Nature.

Morse The code in dots and dashes – Auden is capturing the staccato effect of sudden bursts of song.

in Welsh Again ironic.

their modern family of two Ironic at the expense of the 'planned' families of twentieth century man.

Our Lady's grace The term is religious, but the reference is to Mother Nature too.

heart-rot The parallel is with man – the implication is that the tree is uncared for.

is going smash i.e. bust, bankrupt.

How much they cost A reference to the materialistic society.

Section 3: *Mountains*

Originally published as an Ariel poem in 1954. Six eleven line verses of complex structure and rhyme pattern, with a conversational opening, set the tone. The first verse is rather denigratory of mountains, seeing them as background in paintings, and as various kinds of wall or obstacle. Verse two ranges over the associations of Dracula (for example) and, rather cynically, the dedication of mountaineers; verse three considers journeys, and verse four the world of its own (with associations) of mountains. Verse five considers the 'refuge' and the perspective, while the final verse rather ironically asserts that the poet feels that 'Five minutes on even the nicest mountain/Are awfully long'. It is sometimes difficult to know when Auden is being serious and when he is being flippant, but this poem gives the impression of being an ironic little exercise rather than a 'felt' appraisal.

Masters The classical painters (see *Musée des Beaux Arts*).

Caesar does not rejoice Caesar is here to be equated with a leader of armies who faces difficult terrain.

Dracula By Bram Stoker (1847–1912). It was published in 1897.

habit of the Spiritual i.e. a religious dedication – the image is reinforced by 'their Order' and underlines Auden's irony about mountaineers.

Penrith A market town in Cumberland.

Zurich A canton and large city in Switzerland.

the Flesh i.e. the body.

angels of ice and stone A reference to the height.

Euphemisms Mild expressions for the harsher realities.

O my girl has a goitre Auden is being satirical.

That fled with bronze (The boy) is a physical type belonging to a primitive age.

Black Eagle i.e. an inn.

tarn A small mountain lake.

a real darling Note the slangy, colloquial expression – a light way of saying someone he (perhaps temporarily) loves.

uncatlike A reference to his own lack of balance, familiarity with mountain life.

Section 4: *Lakes*

This too was published in 1953, and again it consists of nine verses, regular but unrhymed, and widely rich in reference, implication and a kind of light, ironic wit. The first sets family scenes and comfort by a lake because of its size, the second asserts that lakes have no evil spirits because of their safe atmosphere. The third verse refers to the the Ascanian Lake (associated with the beginning of the council of churches), and the fourth comes up to date by suggesting that foreign diplomats should discuss peace beside one (perhaps Auden had Lake Geneva in mind). In an ironic fifth verse the poet considers it preferable to drown in a lake (being possessed by its lady) than in the wide impersonal sea, while the sixth has a considered view of reservoirs and fish-pools, and the seventh carries a kind of haunted, Loch Lomond association about it. The eighth is a small assertion of the need to preserve what one has, and the final verse is an imaginative contemplation of the kind of lake the poet might choose (though he knows he won't).

Michigan or Baikal The first is in the United States, on the border with Canada, while the second is in Siberia.

estranging sea See *To Marguerite* (continued) by Matthew Arnold, the last line of which is 'The unplumb'd, salt, estranging sea'.

lacustrine Concerning lakes.

fluvial i.e. found in rivers.

Ascanian At Nicaea, the meeting place of the first council of churches ('The life of Godhead').

widdershins Counter-clockwise.

donkeys pumping as they plod i.e. driving a water-mill.

Poseidon's In Greek mythology, the God of the sea.

Webster's cardinal A reference to Webster's *The Duchess of Malfi* (first performed 1616).

hammer-pond Small storage pool used at a forge.

a visual world/Where beaks are dumb This describes reflections.

savage dogs and man-traps i.e. to keep off those who might interfere.

Fall ... Eden The retreat to Paradise which he will not yield up.

amniotic In the womb, enclosed by the inner membrane. The 'mere' seems to be the womb.

Moraine Debris carried down and deposited by a glacier. The names and the list seem to be Auden's own individual choices.

is ever so comfy The tone here is cliché-ridden, and one feels that Auden is again being satirical.

Section 5: *Islands*

This poem is in short-lined quatrains with alternate lines rhyming. Throughout Auden examines the kinds of people found on islands – saints, pirates, exiled monarchs and criminals, natives, despots like Napoleon, poets, while the final verses dwell on holiday-makers and those who leave for 'a mainland livelihood'. It is a bright and witty poem, exquisitely and, as always, ironically written.

agape love, from the Greek meaning 'brotherly love'.

Hobbes the philosopher (1588–1679) who held that the absolute sovereign power in all matters of right and wrong is vested in the state as the achieved fact of the freeing of the race from savagery.

Napoleon The reference is to his exile on Elba (1815–21).

Sappho The lyric poetess of Greece of the 7th century BC.

Tiberius (42 BC–AD 37) The Roman Emperor in whose reign Christ was crucified.

Section 6: *Plains*

Published in 1954, this is a poem in nine verses of eight lines each in blank verse. The tone is completely conversational, the first verse unequivocally voicing the poet's dislike of plains, the second reinforcing this view; those who live on plains lack direction and inspiration, and as verse succeeds verse this becomes the burthen, reflecting the dullness and sameness of their lives. Others make their mark because they are strong, and the poet expresses his sense of desolation at the contemplation of plains.

pomps of stone where goddesses lay sleeping The reference is to classical mythology, where the gods lived on mountains (i.e. Olympus).

some chisel's kiss i.e. being made into a statue.

the dreamer/Can place his land of marvels i.e. can dream that there is something over the hill.

to seek a million i.e. to make money.

but the Navy A reference to the fact that plain-dwellers sometimes pine for the sea (having no sight of it) and therefore join the navy.

Ovid's charmer ... the quadrilles in Arcady, boy-lord Cupid. For Arcady see note on Arcadia on page 55; Ovid is the great Roman love poet (43 BC–AD 18).

that old grim She According to Spears, Dame Kind.

genera The plural of 'genus': a group of animals or plants having common structural characteristics distinct from other groups and usually subdivided into species.

child-bed ... strawberries i.e. neither will be strong.

How swift to the point of protest i.e. it is easy to catch anyone on plains.

Zeus In Greek mythology, the supreme God.

chamber with Clio In Greek mythology, Clio is the muse of history – the implication here is that it is not the plainsmen who make history.

The Christian cross-bow ... Heathen scimitar The imagery conjures up the Crusades.

fastidious palate i.e. delicate, choosy eater.

Twelve Apostles i.e. those sent forth by Christ to preach the Gospel.

Howling rivers ... Marbles in panic ... Don't-Care Floods of tears ... spilt marbles ... punishments. Nightmarish images recalling the disciplines and miseries of childhood.

Like Tarquin The latter ravished Lucretia, the subject of Shakespeare's poem *The Rape of Lucrece*.

post-coital After sexual intercourse.

Section 7: *Streams*

A longish poem written in quatrains which are unrhymed but which systematically and regularly employ assonance and consonance instead. This is a superbly ironic poem with which to cap the sequence, expressive of warmth and strong identification though of course with the running irony; it was published in 1954 and the tone is colloquial to the point of slanginess, with of course the expected stringency of mind, learning and wit. The first verse is full of love, the second of praise, the third stresses the permanence of the stream throughout history, the fourth and fifth the movement and resilience of streams regardless of landscape. The next three verses designate streams in art and history, while those succeeding define man's relationship to streams and then the poet's memory of his dreaming by one stream and his wakening to 'dearer, water, than ever, your voice'. It is, as Fuller properly suggests, 'almost a sign of grace'.

Air ... earth ... fire Auden is comparing water to the other elements and asserting its superiority.

vocables words, language.

Babel The tower in Shinar (Genesis, 11,9) of many confusing noises.

basalt sill A ledge of igneous rock.

Iseult's ... the willow pash-notes ... Tristram This is the Iseult of Arthurian legend who loved Tristram. Theirs is a story of tragic love, with which the willow is associated, while 'pash-notes' is a deliberate contrast with the high-flown – it merely means 'love-letters'.

Homo Ludens Sporting man.

Huppim ... Muppim Auden has made up these names.

crankle Twist, but note the onomatopoeic effect.

Brahma's son Brahma is a Hindu God. The reference is to the Brahmaputra river, Assam the Indian state into which it flows.

polis A city.

Gaston Paris (1839–1903) French scholar.

Bismarck's siege-guns Bismarck (1815–98) German chancellor. Paris was besieged during the Franco-Prussian War 1870–71, which ended with the surrender of the French and the ceding of Alsace and Lorraine to Germany.

Kisdon Beck A brook or stream.

the mallet i.e. in croquet.

monomaniac i.e. obsessed, with a single idea.

megalith Large stone or monument.

fossil Petrified remains of an animal or vegetable which has become embedded in a rock formation.

armigers i.e. carrying armour.

their holy places i.e. he sees, because he is near the stream, goodness in everything.

Horae Canonicae

Seven poems, the canonical hours 'and the church offices associated with them'. They will be dealt with here singly, and in rather simpler detail than is to be found in either Fuller or Spears, though both these critics have helpful interpretations to offer.

Section 1: *Prime*

The body begins to come alive, waking from sleep, at 6 a.m., the three verses are unrhymed and have sixteen lines each, but again consonance and assonance are evident. The dreams are finished, and man wakes to creation, 'Recalled from the shades to be a seeing being'. The lack of identity is stressed at this time, so that the birth for the new day is symbolic of the birth of man – the first birth. The waking reactions are then described in the second section, with memory, the exertion of will, the resumption of routine, all compared to the beginning – as indeed every day is a beginning. The awareness of the state of sin returns, the awareness too of what the day will bring.

Simultaneously Note the alliteration, almost like the breathing of the waking man.

the vaunt of dawn Unusually put, meaning the 'boast' of dawn.

the nocturnal rummage i.e dreams.

fronde Malcontent party, violent political opposition.

the shades i.e. of the night, dreams.

Its routine of praise and blame Daily life.

Paradise/Lost ... and myself owing a death The fall of man.
share of care ... task ... ask Notice that throughout this
  poem there is a lyrical use made of internal rhyme.

Section 2: *Terce*

Published in 1954, and written in unrhymed verses of thirteen
lines each temptingly close to the form of the sonnet. The time
is 9 a.m., and the individual of the first poem has given way
to three different people starting the day in verse one – the
hangman, the judge, the poet. Verse two moves to the
individual, any individual, praying to get through the coming
day, not to be told off, and perhaps to be lucky. The third verse
focuses on the fact that we (any individual) may participate
in the crucifixion, so that the tone of this verse is deliberately
ironic, the word 'good' carrying the ambiguity that Auden
intends.

the Law that rules the stars i.e. chance, fate.
eclogue A short poem, especially a pastoral dialogue.
the Big Ones Perhaps scientists or dictators in view of the
  context.
repartee i.e. verbal exchange.
Mount Olympus In Greek mythology, the home of the Gods.
Chthonian Of the gods or spirits of the underworld.
a good Friday Ironic – a reference to the crucifixion or just a
  'good' day at the office, for example.

Section 3: *Sext*

This is divided into three distinct parts, and within each a
succession of two-lined unrhymed verses in a conversational
tone. The first part examines the absorbing nature of different
vocations – cooks, surgeons, clerks, for example, – and asserts
that these individuals have ignored the 'appetitive goddesses'
and, if you like, have concentrated on 'doing their own thing'.
They are finally defined as agents – those who fashion
something – and they of course have their parts to play in

the crucifixion. The second part examines the givers of authority, those who rule in one form or another – generals, judges for example – who have the satisfaction of 'being right'. Though the poet suggests that we do not like them, he shows how they have served us, leading us to the death of Christ which 'they' are responsible for. The third part considers the crowd – those who attend the boxing matches and, as here, the crucifixion. Its appetites are served by such a spectacle – what Auden calls its eyes and its mouths.

Rhea, Aphrodite, Demeter, Diana According to Hesiod, the first was one of the Titans, the second is the Greek goddess of love, the third is the daughter of Rhea and sister of Zeus, the fourth the moon goddess.

St Phocas Of Sinope, date uncertain, martyred for his beliefs by soldiers.

St Barbara A Christian martyr of the third century beheaded by her own father.

San Saturnino Probably an Auden coinage, meaning perhaps a 'saint' without joy.

to remain celibate Perhaps because of the temptation of Venus, represented in the Botticelli painting as emerging from a seashell.

Feral Wild, untamed.

a consonant to our names i.e. the initial before our surnames, one of man's distinguishing marks, as in, for example, W. H. (Auden).

Dame Kind One of the three Fates, who governed the lives of all men.

agents The providers of the wherewithal to have a crucifixion.

Fortitudo, Justicia, Nous Endurance, justice, intellect.

basilicas Either buildings used as churches or for lawcourts and assemblies.

divas Prima donnas.

patois Dialect.

The crowd does not see (what everyone sees) Auden is here distinguishing between the crowd as a composite entity acting as one, and the individual who is 'everyone' when he is not in the crowd, and therefore is capable of individual action and appraisal. This distinction is maintained throughout the rest of the section.

epiphany A manifestation, showering forth.

exoskeletons According to Fuller, the reference is to the birds and the bees.

queens i.e. bees (those in authority).

The Prince of this world i.e. Christ.

Section 4: *Nones*

This marks a return to the sixteen-line unrhymed verses, and as the first one reveals, it is now three in the afternoon and the crucifixion is over. Man ponders on his deed in the lazy afternoon and wonders what he will do 'till nightfall'. The second verse explores the disappearance of all those identified with the deed, while in the third the Madonna image is related to the dead Christ, those responsible feeling discarded and abandoned. The fourth is a superb account of the 'stillness/To follow after' acts of love and violence, with the crucifixion as the key act fixed in the memory to which man will always recur. Verse five deals with the renewal of living ('at four') and all the lies and actions and self-indulgence which will follow, and the sixth verse leads us through all the vivid experiences of guilt. The seventh verse is an imaginative series of word-pictures of the watchers at the particular death.

shaman and sybil The Siberian priest and the mouthpiece of a God.

Collect ... wrecked Note again the deliberate internal rhyme, giving the verse a kind of incantatory authority.

The Madonna with the green woodpecker The effect achieved here and in the next two lines is like that of a painting.

Abandoned branch-lines i.e. disused railways. Auden, as we have seen, deliberately mixes past and present.

The spell of the asparagus garden All the references are to the 'vocations', the obsessions we have.

Of the deed i.e. the act, of love or violence, and the reaction which 'they' are now experiencing after the crucifixion.

tramontana The north wind.

quell Suppression.

Abaddon The angel of the bottomless pit.

Belial Incarnation of iniquity and corruption and hence sensuality, one of the fallen angels in Milton's *Paradise Lost*.

On knife edges What follows is a nightmare representation of guilt.

Moors i.e. the fierce people of North Africa.

our Double sits i.e. our other self, perhaps here recording our guilt.

Section 5: *Vespers*

Published in 1955, the time referred to being 6 p.m., each section a short paragraph in prose. The basis is the comparison between the Arcadian and the Utopian ideals, that of the flesh and the spirit in broad terms, with the underlying idea of building a city. The early sections here focus on the flesh (typified by Adam 'his right arm resting for ever on Eve's haunch'), and then the definition through associations of the contrasting views. It is further deepened by modern social and cultural references which contrast the spiritual and material, the cultural and the insensitive. The symbolism comes to be that between Eden and the New Jerusalem, between the innocence of the past and the changes and absolutism of the future. Again at the end there is the return to the crucifixion and its significance.

some vestige of her faceless angel i.e. who has deserted her, is now forgotten.

Sun and Moon supply i.e. man conforms to what is demanded by daytime and night time – work and sleep etc.

Arcadian ... Utopian The first has been defined earlier, the second the imaginary island of supposed political perfection envisaged by Sir Thomas More (1478–1535).

Aquarian ... Scorpion's mouth Reference to the attributes of character and appetite under the signs of the zodiac.

baritoni cattivi Italian, literally 'bad baritones'.

Citadel The fortress of the city.

huge black stones i.e. because unlit.

New Jerusalem The heavenly city, or merely Heaven.

Bellini A reference to the composer (1802–35).

beam-engines This list implies a love of the past.

krum-horns, doppions, sordumes Auden mentions various instruments to indicate the universality of the greeting.

romanesque The architectural style between the classical and gothic periods.

Die Kalte Coldness, frigidity, here personified (German).

august day of outrage The emphasis is on revolution.

hellikins Another Auden coinage, the first part of the word 'hell' indicating destruction.

delations and noyades Impeachments and executions by drowning.

Abel The son of Adam and Eve slain by Cain.

Remus Twin brother of Romulus, and slain by the latter.

Section 6: *Compline*

This is 9 p.m. and the period just before sleep. The form is again the sixteen-lined unrhymed verse, though rich in assonance and consonance. The first verse asserts that at this time everything should make sense, but instead ponders on the meaningless events of the day and the vagaries of memory. The second deals with the confession of the heart and contemplates the heavens, and the third considers the inevitability of the rhythms of life. The last verse quotes from the mass and begs forgiveness for himself and a friend ('dear C'), ending with the reference to the Trinity in terms of 'the dance'.

I can measure but not read i.e. I cannot see into the heart of life, but only measure the passage of time.

cassations Annulments.

to blab To confess.

libera/Me Forgive me.

s-o-b's Generally slang for 'sons of bitches'.

perichoresis Rotation (a theological term).

Section 7: *Lauds*
First of the day's hours of the church, this is what Fuller calls the postscript to the sequence. It is a charming hymn of praise, with the refrain '*In solitude, for company*' expressing the loneliness and yet the togetherness of the individual in prayer or awareness. The form of each verse is a rhyming couplet before the refrain line. The theme appears to be the linking of all in creation.

Thanksgiving for a habitat

About the House, from which this sequence is taken, was published in 1966, and is a witty and varied description of the rooms in Auden's Austrian house. Here each section is examined separately in order to indicate the main themes and treatments as well as the individual styles in which these are expressed.

Section 1: *Prologue The Birth of Architecture (for John Bailey)*
This traces the development from early times through to modern in one long verse, conversational in tone and stressing the effects of the passage of time. All structures emanate from the influence of the 'Old Man' (presumably God or the religious sense) and he goes on to consider what modern man can make 'to puzzle the unborn', for outside there is nature but perhaps man's spiritual sense will see that he continues to build.

Funes ceciderunt ... mihi The lines are fallen unto me in pleasant places; yea I have a goodly heritage (Psalm XVI, verse vi).

gallery-grave ... wren-king ... Low Mass Neolithic burial ... early god ... without music.

carbon clock i.e. changes in the earth, a recording of time in terms of periods like the ice age, stone age and so on.

Bicycle Age i.e. of the poet's own youth.

Stonehenge The most famous of the stone-circles on Salisbury Plain.

Chartres Cathedral Thirteenth century Gothic of celebrated design, with outstanding, stained-glass windows.

Acropolis The rocky eminence which dominates Athens.

Blenheim The famous palace, seat of the Duke of Marlborough, named after his famous victory over the French (1704).

the Albert Memorial The monument in memory of Queen Victoria's consort in Kensington Gardens.

concrete or grapefruit According to Fuller, this symbolizes technology.

that Immortal Commonwealth i.e. Nature.

Section 2: *Thanksgiving for a Habitat* (*for Geoffrey Gorer*)
A poem in quatrains, unrhymed but with significant consonance, which looks at who is going to live in a particular place. Auden examines his own, and considers the home that spiders make too, aware of his own difference and separateness as he works in his house. He contemplates too death in his home, whether atomic or pedestrian, but the tone is lightly humorous, certainly as if he is enjoying the exercise. His independence of social responsibility ends with the assertion that his home is 'a place/I may go both in and out of'.

who got laid/by a sacred beast The reference is obviously to classical mythology, and one is reminded of Yeats's 'Leda and the Swan'.

a press lord W. R. Hearst, the American newspaper magnate.

San Simeon The palatial residence which Randolph Hearst built for himself.

their lethal bicycle chains i.e. weapons of violence with which to assault the adulterer (or the husband).

Hetty Pegler's Tump Neothilic barrow at Uley in the Cotswolds.

Schönbrunn Viennese palace, formerly the residence of the Emperors of Austria.

Proustian A reference to the famous French novelist Marcel Proust, author of *A La Recherche du Temps Perdu*, technically one of the most influential writers of this century.

Jacksonian Perhaps an ironic reference to Andrew Jackson

(1767–1845), President of the United States who often used the Presidential veto.

Darwin (1809–82) *His Origin of the Species by Natural Selection* (1859) revolutionized scientific thought and established a theory of evolution.

clone Group (of plants) directly descended from one individual.

a transplant from overseas Remember that Auden lived in Austria.

Linnaeus Swedish botanist (1707–78).

Amphibia Frogs, toads and similar creatures which can breathe in air or water.

Arachnids i.e. the class of spiders, scorpions and mites.

Hitler The German dictator responsible for the spread of Nazism and the Second World War. All the evidence points to his death in a bunker in Berlin in 1945.

esophagus The canal from the mouth to the stomach, the gullet.

smidge Presumably meaning 'a small amount'.

nano-second A unit of time, equal to 1,000-millionth of a second.

c.c. Cubic centimetre.

giga-death Perhaps a widespread death, for example owing to atomic war.

blunderbuss Ancient short gun firing many balls.

bailiwick District under the jurisdiction of a Bailiff.

toft-and-croft Homestead and enclosed piece of land.

Section 3: *The Cave of Making* (*In Memoriam, Louis Macneice*)

Louis MacNeice Was Auden's friend (they collaborated on *Letters from Iceland*), a considerable poet himself, who died in 1963. This is in memory of MacNeice, and goes back in time in a free-flowing blank verse narrative. Auden is writing about places where things – like poems – are created, where 'all is subordinate/Here to a function'. The key to it is silence. It is Auden's own room, and he wishes that he could have shown it to MacNeice; thereafter he traces their friendship and the changes in the wider world (like those made by Stalin and Hitler). The poet even takes comfort that the dead MacNeice can always be with him, and then writes of poetry itself. It is a moving and intimate tribute.

Weland's stithy Weland was the hero of Teutonic myth who amassed wealth at his famous forge.

Olivetti portable A typewriter.

videnda Things worth seeing.

Donegal County in the North West of Ireland.

Carolingian The second French dynasty founded by Charlemagne.

Bavaria The largest of the German states, about the size of Scotland.

Horace's The Roman poet (65–8 BC)

porphyry-born This is hard rock, used to make vessels to hold liquids in former days. The allusion is to a person born in the upper stratum of society.

Malory Sir Thomas, who flourished in the 15th century, celebrated for his prose work on the Arthurian legends, *Morte D'Arthur*.

numinous Attraction and awe, all powerful here, meaning that the lord of the manor was effectively god in terms of power.

Cosmic Model i.e. the 'model' for the universe – Nazism.

Stalin and Hitler For the note on the latter see p.73. After the exile of Trotsky Stalin gradually assumed power in Russia, a power which he held until his death in 1953.

last Fall Autumn.

the Country of Unconcern Death.

Poems ... The Burning Perch Volumes published by MacNeice.

Symposium Contributions or discussion on one subject by a number of people.

juggins Fool.

Baroque Prince A state ruler in central Europe, 16th-18th centuries.

this unpopular art i.e. poetry.

'done' i.e. explored as a tourist.

Tolstoy The great Russian novelist (1828–1910). He has to be 'abridged' because of the length of, for example, *War and Peace*.

Nietzsche (1844–1900) The German philosopher whose doctrine was that strength alone is admirable and weakness the only vice. He exerted a great influence.

plebs The common people.

optimates Roman aristocrats, literally 'the best men'.

Talleyrand The great French statesman (1754–1838).

Goethe German writer and philosopher (1749–1832).

that frontier i.e. of death.

mawk and hooey i.e. sentiment and rubbish.

dear shade i.e. spirit.

Section 4: *Down There* (*for Irving Weiss*)

Four blank-verse stanzas about the associations of cellars; they began as caves, and now are the foundations on which we rest, keeping alcohol and conserves, for example, safe. Auden's whimsy in the last two verses plays on their permanence, their lack of offence – not lived in, they don't resent being left.

Great Cold Winter.

key-cold cloak Fine image, personifying and domesticating in its emphasis.

creepy-crawlies Insects – notice that Auden adopts the tone of the child sent down into the cellar.

Who seldom visit others i.e. rarely go down (into the cellar).

Section 5: *Up There* (*for Anne Weiss*)

Three verses, in the same form as the previous poem, about the attic. Generally women store things in attics, which is a lumber room having no particular dignity, but it is used by children both as retreat and for imaginative adventure. This is a light poetic exercise.

galoshes Overshoes for protection against the rain or snow.

plenum Space filled with matter.

eyrie Perched high (as an eagle's nest).

Section 6: *The Geography of the House* (*for Christopher Isherwood*)

Written in eight-line verses, short lines running into each other, with a simple rhyme scheme and a lyrical flow, this is a description of what Auden would certainly call the 'loo'. It is witty, both subtly and crudely coarse, and examines both punningly and otherwise the subject of excretion. The permanence of excretion is stressed, from the cradle (or potty) to the grave, and in fact the range of reference and association makes this a lightweight but intellectually stimulating poem.

white-tiled cabin The irony is apparent, for the term employed here is a euphemism.

This i.e. excretion.

Dump Slang for opening the bowels.

Luther The great Protestant founder of the Reformation (1483–1546).

Rodin The famous statue of the Thinker by the eminent French sculptor (1840–1918).

ur-act Primitive, original.

De-narcissus-ized en-/during excrement Auden's humour, coarse, at attempts to produce something devoid of self-love, and compared here to excrement.

Freud The great founder of the study of psycho-analysis. (1856–1939)

For Night Deposits ... firm or liquid ... soft or hard A punning sequence on excrement.

Bowels of compassion A phrase synonymous with 'pity'.

weak-sphinctered i.e. unable to control the bowel or bladder.

Higher Thought i.e. meditation.

Major/Prophet taken short i.e. needing suddenly to visit the lavatory.

Swift Dean Swift (1667–1745) the author of *Gulliver's Travels*.

St Augustine The greatest of the Latin fathers of the church (354–430).

Manichees Those who ascribe the universe to two antagonistic principles, for example God and the Devil.

Section 7: *Encomium Balnei (for Neil Little)*

The title means 'In Praise of the Bathroom or Bathing(?)', and just as the bathroom is itself an escape, so is the subject matter of this poem, which is written in a whimsical, conversational free verse. There follows an account of the washed and unwashed in time ('Shakespeare probably stank'), the size and diminishing of it in modern times, the influence perhaps of the saints, ending this section in praise of privacy. One can feel important in a bath, can sing, and feel happy. This summary does scant justice to the ingenuity of Auden's treatment.

hydropathy Generally, medical treatment by internal and external application of water.

Faith and Works The Puritan ideal that what you do matters as much as what you believe.

Le Grand Monarque Louis XIV (1638–1715).

hirsute Covered with hair.

caracallan acreage A reference to the large baths built by Caracella in Rome in the third century AD.

tepidarium's Intermediate room of moderate temperature in Roman baths.

St Anthony (251–351) the anchorite who spent twenty years of his life in a lonely ruin.

Broadway Famous New York thoroughfare known particularly for its theatres.

caul The membrane enclosing the foetus (child).

mallarmesque/syllabic fog A reference to Stephane Mallarmé, the French poet (1842–98) and his use of bizarre words and general obscurity.

The Pilgrim's Way ... the War Path Presumably, two different definitions of life.

Von Hügel's hoggers and lumpers Von Hügel (1852–1925) was a Roman Catholic writer on religion. He settled in England in 1871.

Section 8: *Grub First, Then Ethics* (*Brecht*) (*for Margaret Gardiner*) We are back to the sixteen-line verse, but the introduction of occasional rhymes gives the poem a musical lilt. In the first verse Auden talks of what could be said about man to Plato, by the end coming to 'Here/is the place where we cook'. The second introduces the American kitchen in Lower Austria (his home), the third elaborates in description of it. The fourth is finally, after considerable and diverting wit, in praise of an omelette, while the fifth examines gluttony in fiction and in life and casts a glance at the frustrations of those who prepare and serve food. The last verse considers that the city is sustained by the good dinners which enable men to 'hold her Thermopylae'.

Brecht (1898–1956).Famous German Marxist playwright.

Plato The great Athenian philosopher, (427–347 BC).

anthropos mankind.

Telford The celebrated engineer and bridge-builder (1757–1834).

for a dig at Athens i.e. to show that we are superior in this respect (to Plato's time).

Age of Poise i.e. royalty or aristocracy or the rich.

New Cnossos Knossos, the site in Crete which yielded many discoveries of the ancient world.

birthday-button The navel.

banausics People employed on mechanical labour.

Mozart The eminent composer born in Salzburg (1756–91).

neotene A species in which the period of immaturity is indefinitely prolonged.

God is edible A reference to the Holy Communion.

trencherman i.e. heavy eater.

forum Public place.

meres break Lakes or ponds flood.

Thermopylae The famous pass where Leonidas and his Spartans tried to hold off the Persian hordes under Xerxes (480 BC)

Section 9: *For Friends Only* (*for John and Teckla Clark*)
Eight verses of six lines each, unrhymed. Each line, as Fuller has noted, consists of either five or seven lines. The first verse commemorates the friends staying for the week-end, the third details some of the things likely to occur, the fourth talks of confessing worries, the fifth of the difficulties of the language of friendship. The sixth says that the room will always be ready, the seventh mentions food (biscuits and a bottle of

mineral water), and the eighth verse bids the guests goodnight in their 'guest-room'. Again, out of virtually nothing Auden has made an entertaining conversational poem which evinces his ready kindness, compassion and wit.

cognates Having the same linguistic family.
galimatias Confused or meaningless talk, rigmarole.
Tum-Tum's i.e. (the rule) of the stomach.
Felicissima notte Sleep well.

Section 10: *Tonight at Seven-Thirty (for M. F. K. Fisher)*
Six verses of varied length line but a regular rhyme-scheme, carefully worked out and sustained. The first describes animal life before moving on to examine how man does honours to the feast; this melts into verse two which examines man's ability to entertain in various primitive times, verse three speculates on the right number (deploring mass banquets) and verse four lays down certain rules; verse five continues this, and verse six indicates the ideal situation and balance for dinner and the ensuing conversation. Auden deploys many of his verbal tricks in this romp through table-talk – in fact it might be said that the poem itself *is* a form of table-talk.

pack-hunters i.e. animals (like wolves) which hunt together.
en famille i.e. as a family.
supererogatory Doing more than is required by duty.
Glaciation The ice-age.
Long Pig English equivalent of the words used by cannibals to describe human flesh.
Leviathan The sea-monster mentioned in the Bible.
crenellated Furnished with battlements or loopholes.
instanter At once.
comity Courtesy.
flosculent Typical unusual Auden usage, here meaning 'flowery'.
cenacle A supper room, especially that in which the Last Supper was eaten by Jesus and his disciples.
baker's dozen Thirteen.
rundle Presumably a reference to the Round Table.

holy Zodiac number Twelve.

curmurr Note the onomatopoeic effect.

maltalents i.e. whose talents are badly balanced.

gnostic i.e. having esoteric spiritual knowledge.

cloop Note the fine onomatopoeic quality.

olamic silence Belonging to a vast period or age.

Section 11: *The Cave of Nakedness (for Louis and Emmie Kronenberger)*

This is a blank verse description of the 'habitat' of the body, the bedroom, with the now expected associations both literary and historical and spiritual and personal. Bed-sitting rooms are condemned, as are dormitories, and then Auden becomes fluently autobiographical. The last section is given over to the contemplation of the night, its fears and sounds right through to the ultimate re-awakening. Somehow, though there is a certain loneliness inherent in it, it is a tender poem, expressing a warmth of love.

Don Juan The legendary lover and the subject of a long poem by Lord Byron.

unmythical i.e. real.

baldachined and nightly-redamselled Richly brocaded and canopied and each night having different girls (for the Emperor).

effable data The opposite of 'ineffable', which means unutterable or too great for words.

bona fide Genuine.

Edwardian England The reign of Edward VII (1901–10). Auden was born in 1907.

the transit i.e. of going to bed.

colloquia of Derbies and Joans Discussions between old married couples.

perks Advantages.

day-wester Sunset.

never got to Italy Never travelled, did not go on the Grand Tour.

disband Break up, disperse.

Gospel Makers Matthew, Mark, Luke, John.

fire, nightmare Auden is cataloguing the fears of the night which often beset us.

Holy Four i.e. the Gospel Makers.

avian orchestra The dawn chorus (getting ready).

Country of Consideration i.e. awake, when we 'think'.

Section 12: *The Common Life (for Chester Kallman)*

This is in praise of the living room in a number of unrhymed quatrains; various room styles are considered, and the room which is shared by Auden and Kallman (to whom the poem is dedicated) is particularized. The awareness of the give and take of their friendship, the fact that they have survived both the world and each other, is an essential part of the poem. There is more description of the room and of their habits, and its self-contained nature is emphasized (every home should be a fortress), and the poem moves to the conclusion that love is more important than truth.

you (Thou, rather) An underlining of courtesy and consideration.

its dogmas i.e. its standards of taste.

checks Cheques.

quizzing ours i.e. looking closely. Sherlock Holmes, Conan Doyle's famous investigator from Baker Street, normally deduced the habits of the people he met from certain give-away signs in their appearances or where they lived.

the burly-back of a slave Note once again Auden's recurrence to the past.

clerisy The class of learned men, scholars.

conversational tics and larval habits Probably oddities of conversation and perhaps movements while asleep.

cater-cousins Intimates, on good or familiar terms.

Naples Bambino A child – a painting here.

Strauss and Stravinsky The first the German composer, the second the Russian composer.

the Dark Lord ... animivorous chimeras Fears and the many forms they take.

The ogre will come in any case Notice that Auden has returned to the world of the fairy story in order to illustrate his point.

Joyce James Joyce (1882–1941) the author of *Ulysses*.

the Letter Of the law (or of good taste).

Revision questions on W. H. Auden

1 Compare and contrast any *two* of Auden's shorter poems.

2 By close reference to *three* or more poems, indicate Auden's variety within the sonnet form.

3 Write an essay on Auden's use of imagery in any *three* poems.

4 Write an appreciation of any of Auden's poems which reflect his political concern.

5 By close reference to any *three* or *four* poems, indicate the variety of Auden's humour.

6 Write a commentary on 'The Sea and the Mirror', bringing out clearly the nature of Auden's achievement.

7 By close reference to any *two* poems, show how important the word 'love' is in any appreciation of Auden.

8 In what ways is Auden 'irreverent'? You should refer to any *three* or *four* poems in your answer.

9 Write an essay on the spiritual content of Auden's verse.

10 In what ways is Auden's poetry lyrical? You may refer to any three or four poems in your answer.

11 What are Auden's main concerns in 'Horae Canonicae'?

12 How far is an appreciation of art *or* music important in our understanding of Auden's poetry?

13 Write an essay on Auden's use of classical associations in his poetry.

14 Write an appreciation of any two of the poems in 'Thanksgiving for a Habitat'.

15 Write an essay on Auden's use of the colloquial or conversational or both in his verse.

16 In what ways is Auden's poetry esoteric? Refer to a range of poems in your answer.

17 What are Auden's chief likes and dislikes judging from his verse? You should refer to a number of poems in your answer.

18 Write an essay defending Auden from the charge of being needlessly obscure.

19 How important is the conception of the 'quest' in Auden's poetry?

20 Which of Auden's poems do you find the most moving and why?

21 Write an essay on Auden's sense of *place* in his verse.

22 In what ways may Auden's verse be considered *ironic*? Refer to a range of poems in your answer.

23 Do you regard Auden as a cynical poet? Give reasons for your answer.

24 In what ways is there evidence of compassion and humanity in Auden's poetry? Give reasons for your answer.

25 Write an essay on Auden's treatment of death in any *two* poems.